Coming Up Down Home

A MEMOIR OF A SOUTHERN CHILDHOOD

Coming Up Down Home

A MEMOIR OF A SOUTHERN CHILDHOOD

Cecil Brown

 THE ECCO PRESS

The Ecco Press
100 West Broad Street
Hopewell, NJ 08525
Published simultaneously in Canada by
Penguin Books Canada Ltd., Ontario
Printed in the United States of America
Designed by Debby Jay
First Edition

Library of Congress Cataloging-in-Publication Data

Brown, Cecil, 1943–
    Coming up down home : a memoir of a southern childhood / Cecil
Brown.
        p.   cm. — (The Dark Tower series)
    ISBN 0-88001-293-5
    1. Brown, Cecil, 1943–   —Homes and haunts—Southern States.
2. Afro-Americans—Southern States—Social life and customs.
3. Afro-American authors—20th century—Biography.   4. Brown, Cecil,
1943–   —Biography—Youth.   5. Sharecroppers—Southern States.
I. Title.   II. Series.
PS3552.R6853Z464   1993
813′.54—dc20
    [B]   93-20286
                                                                        CIP

The text of this book is set in Century Schoolbook

For Aunt Amanda and Uncle Lofton
My Mother and Father
My Sisters and Brothers
. . . and Randi

Contents

Coming Up Down Home

A MEMOIR OF A SOUTHERN CHILDHOOD

PART ONE

Pickaninny

Back in Black mountain
A child will smack your face
Babies cryin for liquor
And all the birds sing bass
—BESSIE SMITH

Chapter 1

~~~~~~

"**D**on't you remember your mother?" Uncle Lofton said. I lifted my head and looked at her again.

She was tall, thin, and pretty. She was much too pretty to be my mother.

As she came nearer, Aunt Amanda, nudging me behind the neck, said, "Ain't you going to say hello to your mother?"

Several members of the family were standing around watching us.

I took a step toward her and smelled perfume. Then a memory, and an uneasiness in my stomach, stopped me. I remembered my mother leaving the house, and my running behind her crying her name and begging her to take me with her. She stopped and threw her high heel shoe at me; I still remembered the throbbing puncture on my head where the shoe hit.

"She ain't my mother," I said, turning to look back at Aunt Amanda. Aunt Amanda was smiling, and when she smiled, I could see the gold tooth in the back of her mouth. She was a squat black woman dressed in a polka-dot dress with a wide white collar and wore a familiar flat, wide-brimmed Sunday school hat.

Aunt Amanda cooked for me and my brother, who was a year younger than me; she bought us clothes from Sears Roebuck, made us shirts from feed sacks. From the white people she worked for, she brought home food and surprises. Sometimes she would get mad if we disobeyed her, expressing her disapproval with a grunt capable of different meanings depending on the intonation. My brother and I knew all of them. If anybody was going to be my mother, it would be Aunt Amanda.

"She ain't my mother," I blurted out louder to Aunt Amanda. "You my mamma!"

"Boy, ain't you gonna hug yo own . . . mamma!" somebody else demanded.

"He act lak he doan know her!" said another member of the family.

My mother kneeled down beside me.

"Morris," she said gently, "don't you remember me?" Now the smell of perfume was so strong and the voice was so deeply familiar that a wave of sadness swept over me. She touched my head. I wanted to cry, but held back my tears. My little brother, my charge since my father and mother went away, must never be allowed to see me cry.

"Ain't you glad to see me?" she asked again. I watched her face now. I watched her red-painted lips. And then she laughed.

"Go on," Uncle Lofton said sternly. I felt it was my duty to go to my mother then.

"Yes, I'm glad to see you," I said finally.

"Well, isn't that *pretty*," Aunt Amanda said from behind me.

I began to watch her, sidelong, to see if she was behaving like she was our mother.

"Oh, he's so cute!" Aunt Ruby said, glancing at my greasy laid-back naps. "The way he wears his hair!"

"Oh, he real particular about his clothes," I heard Aunt Amanda say to my mother, as if she were talking to a stranger about the habits of a pet. I conveyed my suspicion to my brother in a glance . . . and then looked down at her shoes. They were too fancy, too high.

"He wants everything ironed," Aunt Amanda said. "Both of them do." She showed our mother how well-mannered we were.

Buckcaesar, the family dog, stirred under the table. I turned from my mother and Aunt Amanda and bent down to play with the dog. Buckcaesar was such a big dog that my brother and I used to ride him like a horse. He understood me and my brother. We used to fall asleep with him in a shade tree behind the house. I wanted very much to be with him and not with my mother.

He was wet underneath. His moist, bushy belly meant that Uncle Lofton had just come back from hunting. My mother didn't smell as nice as Buckcaesar. I preferred the natural smell to her perfume. Pulling at the shaggy wet hair, I began to laugh in so

4

unmannerly a fashion that Uncle Lofton seized me by the neck and hauled me from my sanctuary beneath the table to face my mother.

"Lissen, boy, yo mamma is here! Now act like somebody!"

When I turned away, my mother came over to me and tried to pick me up. My mood had changed regarding her. I wanted very much to be nice to her, to be hugged by her.

I shrugged my shoulders, shaking her hands off.

"You dawg, you!" I said to her when she tried to touch me again. I muttered this, sort of laughing to myself. My brother heard me, and we looked at each other and laughed.

"Now, you know that ain't nice," she said.

"Oh, ain't he grown?" Aunt Amanda asked. "Don't call yo mamma that. You and your brother, sing yo song for yo mamma now!"

For this occasion, Aunt Amanda had taught us to sing "My Bonnie Lies Over the Ocean," with the somber lyrics of "My father is in the mountains. My mother is gone away. Bring back my father and mother to me!"

When I had asked Aunt Amanda why we should sing that song, she said so we wouldn't feel so lonely when we sung it. And when you see your mother, Uncle Lofton said, you should sing that for her and she'll feel good too. We had practiced all day and again before saying our prayers.

Instead of singing the song, though, I turned on Aunt Amanda too, something I'd never done before.

"You dawg, you!"

Over my voice she said to my mother, "Oh, they sing so purtty. Both of them so smart!"

"Now shut up, Morris, you hear," Grammy Commie said, and I turned on her too.

Grammy looked like a combination of a white woman and an Indian. I was afraid of her whiteness—her mother Dana had been born in the Oakland Plantation and was the daughter of one of the white planters.

"You dawg, you!"

Grammy Commie drew back her hand. I knew that she would hit me. Grammy Commie didn't play. She'd hit you hard enough to cripple you, without even thinking.

"Boy, I'll knock you into the middle of next week!" she squeaked in her high, shaky voice, lunging for me. I vaulted out of her grasp and took refuge under the table again.

From my asylum I heard sounds of laughter from Uncle Sugarboy and others. But I could tell by my mother's solemn tone that she was upset.

"Lofton, what's wrong with him?" she asked. She sounded critical, I suppose, of how he had reared me and my brother. A great presumption on her part.

Uncle Lofton said, "Well, everybody treats him lak a dawg. He don't know nothing else."

"B-b-but, I-I-tell you one t-t-thing," Uncle Sugarboy stuttered, "hit's a wise child that knows his mother is in a-a-bathing suit!" They all thought that was so funny. All of them except Uncle Lofton.

Even though he had taken responsibility to raise me and my brother and was the only father I could remember, I hated him too at this moment.

I saw his face appear under the table.

"Come on out, son," he said. "It's all right now."

"Naw," I shouted back.

He reached out his hand to me.

"Don't touch me, you dawg, too."

"Don't say that, son," he said.

"Dawg!"

"Now if you keep on saying it, I'm going to whip you," he said.

"Dawg!"

"Oh, Morris," my mother said, trying again, "come to me."

"No! You dawg!"

Uncle Lofton pulled his belt off slowly, hoping to frighten me. Yes, I was afraid. But I didn't want to show them. Did he think I would shut up just because he was going to beat me?

Uncle Lofton, who was no blood kin to our family, was the one I felt closest to, and he was the only person everybody believed could raise me and my brother. I don't know why. But his being a no-blood relative made him the perfect person to take responsibility for us, to spank and chastise us.

Uncle Lofton's face, open and honest and wonderful, appeared under the table again. To explain his long straight "good" hair and long nose, like white people's, and his even brown skin, he told us he was an Indian. He was actually one-fourth Cherokee Indian, but his "good hair" and straight nose probably came from

6

his grandmother, Molly Ward, who was a straight-out white woman.

"Come on, son," he pleaded again.

"Dawg!" I said again. I didn't know why I kept saying it, but I just did. I wanted to take that smile from my mother's lips and destroy our carefully orchestrated reunion.

"Now you stop that, boy," Uncle Lofton said.

"Dawg!"

Aunt Amanda grunted, "Hummm!" but I still said, "Dawg!"

Uncle Lofton caught my leg and pulled me out.

He raised the belt and brought it down lightly over my leg, and I screamed out louder than ever, "Dawg!" He whacked me again but I screamed louder this time, giving him no choice but to smack me again.

When my mother saw how determined I was, she looked upset and helpless, which suited me just fine. I wanted her to know how long I had waited for her to come back to me and my brother, although it was too late.

She tried to console me again, but I screamed and cried as loud as I could. Uncle Lofton beat me until he couldn't beat me any longer, and yet my spite was not a bit lessened.

"Now don't you call you mother a dawg again," he said, his own voice shaky and his breath panting. "Don't let me hear you say dawg again."

"Hit him! He can't sassy grown-ups! You ought to get a sweet gum switch and fan his behind for him good. That's what I'd do!" Gramma Commie was yelling. "He so grown, he already smelling himself!"

Sweat was already pouring from Uncle Lofton's shirt. He stopped, exhausted. "I'm not going to hit him anymore," he said, and then he looked down at me. "I can't beat you no more now."

My anger was metaphysical. Hit me, I don't care. Kill me, kill . . . go ahead . . . kill me! I don't care!

I wanted to say *dawg* again but my breath was too quick and I was crying too loud. I crawled under the table, beyond their reach.

When I finally got my breathing together and prepared myself for another round, I discovered that they had all turned the conversation to another topic, although they were still glancing at me out of the corner of their collective eye.

I got up from under the table and stood up.

7

"Now, Morris, be a *nice* boy," my mother said.

"If y-you don't beat him now," Uncle Sugarboy said, "h-h-he'll walk all over you one day, Lofton!"

"That's enough," Uncle Lofton said as he dropped his belt. "I can't beat that child no mo." I loved him for letting me win.

". . . You—" and I was about to say *dawg* again when I saw Uncle Lofton raise his belt again, yet I was determined I would not bow to them.

So I looked down at Buckcaesar and then raised my head and shouted, ". . . You *Buckcaesar!* You *Buckcaesar!*"

That broke the tension, and everybody laughed.

"He wouldn't say 'dawg' cause he seed that L-L-Lofton was gonna put-put-put that belt on his-his-his behind, so he-he-he called Dorothy Buckcaesar, but as far-far-far as he-he-he is concern, she's still a dawg!" Uncle Sugarboy explained. "That boy is smart!"

Immediately my mother hugged me and my brother.

Chapter 2

‹‹‹‹‹‹‹‹‹‹‹‹‹‹‹‹‹‹‹‹‹‹‹‹‹‹‹‹‹‹‹‹‹‹

We drove in Uncle Lofton's car from my grandmother's house to Uncle Lofton's house, which was located a few miles away, on the backside of the town, in a place called Outback. The smell of Aunt Amanda's sausages crept into the room, and the next thing I saw was big plates of grits being brought in from the kitchen and placed before me at the table.

"Now, you and your brother go on and eat," Aunt Amanda said. But even though I was hungry, I couldn't get over the trauma of seeing my mother again.

"Hey! Hey! *Y'all!*" a loud, masculine voice bellowed out. I turned from the table and saw a tall black man in the kitchen door.

Mr. Roy Melvin came in the back door and greeted everybody. He lived across the ditch back in the hollow with his wife Mrs. Suzanne and their eight children. "How them *boys* doing?" he asked when he was finished with his greetings, glancing over at me and my brother.

I liked Mr. Roy Melvin better than anybody. He worked on the railroad with Uncle Lofton and had two boys the same age as my brother and I. On the way home from working on the railroad, he would play his harmonica. My brother and I, hearing his music, would ask permission from Aunt Amanda to go meet him and would run the two miles to greet him. He would play a tune for us called "Fox Chase," and we would dance as fast as we could. "Go, boys, *go*," he'd always say.

He had his harp with him. I looked at him from the table. I just wanted him to play something so my brother and I could dance.

"Mr. Roy Melvin, play the 'Fox Chase' for us," I said to him. "Fox Chase" was fast, like dogs after a coon, and we never tired of dancing to it.

"Eat yo *breakfast*," Aunt Amanda said. "Ain't gonna be no *dancin* in here!"

"Yeah, we takin these boys up in the mountains to see their real daddy," Uncle Lofton told him.

"Morris and Knee," he said now, glancing over at my mother, "going up there to see your daddy, huh? Now y'all gots to get on the road, you ain't got time to dance now. Though when y'all gets back, I'm gonna play the 'Fox Chase' for you, okay?"

"Yessir!" I shouted, promising anything to hear him play.

"Now, you remember to tell yo daddy, I'm waiting on him to get on back here, and help me out wit this coon hunting." He threw his head back and laughed, the way only Mr. Roy Melvin could do.

"Okay," I said, puzzled. I didn't understand that we were going to see our father. Perhaps this visit to our father was the reason our mother was here? I realized that I had behaved very badly for a boy who was being reunited with his real parents.

"Now go on and eat yo breakfast, so we can get goin," he said.

After we ate, there was a knock at the door.

Another tall black man walked in, smiling. Our mother was excited to see him. I thought that this was our father. But Aunt Amanda explained to us he was our Uncle Jack.

Uncle Jack kneeled down to me.

"Do you want to see yo papa?"

When I didn't answer, he said, "Well, let's go! I want to see him!"

"Good-bye, now!" Mr. Roy Melvin said, standing on the plank of board that lay across the ditch.

"Bye, Roy! Good-bye, Mr. Roy Melvin!" we yelled from the car, as Uncle Lofton pulled down the dirt road.

I sat in the backseat between my mother and the window, right behind Uncle Lofton. "Where we going, Uncle Lofton?" I asked.

"We going to see some mountains," he said.

"Big mountains? Where?"

"In the Shenandoah Valley. In Virginia."

"Is it far?"

"Almost half a day by car."

"Why?"

10

"Don't you want to see the mountains?" he answered.

"Yes!"

"And don'tcha want to see your daddy?" Aunt Amanda said. I looked at her and then at my mother sitting next to Uncle Jack. After going through what I had with seeing my mother, I wasn't so sure. But the more I looked at her, the better I liked her. My brother was already in her arms asleep.

Uncle Lofton drove along the dirt road that led to the unpaved highway, passed the mailbox, and turned right. When we had driven half a mile, he slowed down and pulled off the road and stopped the car in front of Buster Jacob's place.

Buster Jacob was a big, bright, light-skinned man who called himself an Indian. Nobody disputed his claim to his face, although there was a lot of talk about it behind his back. Some people said he was just another redbone nigger.

As the car stopped, I saw him leaning against his shop—he had a small, whitewashed, shingled shed from which he sold soda pops, nabs, peanuts, candy, chewing tobacco, and cigarettes. It was here, on the steps, that the men in our village would gather to talk about what they really felt. There was never a wedding or funeral that didn't end up here as conversation. Gossip was spawned and maintained; reputations were created and destroyed. Across from the store, or "shop," as they called it, was the back porch of Mr. Buster Jacob's large white house. And it was on this porch that the women would sit under quilts with Mr. Buster Jacob's Indian wife and create their own gossip, rivaling the men's. Nearly everybody in the community came to this store at least once a day to get the news and to leave messages. We had our own impromptu mayor, and our own city hall in the area between Buster Jacob's back porch and the steps of his shop.

"Hey, Lofton," Mr. Buster said. "Y'all goin up there to see Cuffy." Cuffy was the name my father's friends called him.

"Yeah, we goin to see him," Uncle Lofton said. "Give me a pack of Camels. And give these boys a soda pop."

Buster Smith came out of the shop with a box of cigarettes.

"Lofton, I ain't gonna charge you for these," he said. "I want you to give Cuffy these cigarettes for me. Tell him . . ." He said something which I didn't hear and laughed. I waved at him and Mr. Buster Jacob. I began to feel the old sense of foreboding and dread whenever I thought of my father.

When we had all piled into the car, Buster Jacob, his big belly

11

supporting his lazy, red, swollen hand, called out, "Now, don't forget to tell Cuffy what I said!"

As the car drove along Route 74–78, I began reading the outdoor advertisements out loud. Reading these advertisements was the way I studied the culture which I would have to know well in order to survive.

Ethyl Gasoline! United Gas serving the Gulf South! . . . Which Twin has the *Toni!* . . . *I. W. Harper*-precious-aged-bottled-in-bond! *Chesterfield*—the best cigarette for YOU to smoke! Buy the most distinguished luxury car in the field . . . Frazer! *Buick* Roadmaster with Dynaflow Drive! *DeSoto* . . . The Car Designed with You in Mind! *Packard*—the last word in automatic, no-shift control!

Strange brand names flowed by the highway. The light blue sky faded out to white cotton balls.

"What does that say?" Uncle Lofton asked me, glancing back at me and then at my mother. I began to feel better about my mother, and the pain from that morning began to fade away.

"That boy can read already," he said to her. My mother was crying. Why was she crying? Uncle Jack was not crying and was as quiet as a big black rock.

We rode along the road. When we saw a sign, I'd read it out loud, and Uncle Lofton would admire my erudition. He could not read it himself, but he aided me by asking and approving the response as he drove along the Shenandoah Valley.

I looked at the green mountains. "Uncle Lofton, look at the mountains!"

"They big, ain't they?" he asked.

"Is my daddy up in the mountains?"

"Yes, he sho is."

"Why is he in the mountains?" I asked. I looked at my mother but she was crying again. As we drove along, I saw a group of men working on the side of the road. One of them had a gun.

"Are they soldiers, Uncle Lofton?"

"They soldiers alright," Uncle Jack said.

"Is my daddy a soldier?"

"He a soldier, but he ain't in no army," Uncle Jack said.

I didn't understand. How could he be a soldier and not be a soldier in an army?

Uncle Lofton and Uncle Jack started talking rapidly about other things I couldn't understand. Uncle Lofton would always call A. J. Harris the "boss man," but when we were a long ways away from our town, he called him "Jack Harris," making it sound like "Jack-ass!"

When they talked about Geechie Collins, who lived in the alley in our town, Uncle Jack said, "I wouldn't trust that nigger as far as I could throw an elephant."

"The man is just not trustworthy," Uncle Lofton said.

"Is my real daddy a trust-tee?" I asked.

Aunt Amanda had told me our father was a "trust-tee," and I thought a "trust-tee" was something like being a "general" or a "captain."

"Is who a trust-tee?" Uncle Lofton asked.

"Cuffy, my other daddy."

"Yes, he is a trustee. Where did you hear that?"

"Aunt Amanda told me," I said.

"That boy don't forget nuthin you tell him!" Uncle Lofton said. "Nuthin!"

"What does that say?"

"Dunlap Tires!—" I said, catching an advertisement on a billboard that swished by.

"Ha, ha! See, that boy is smart!" Uncle Lofton said.

I wanted to stop to get some soda. When I saw a beautiful bar and restaurant, I pleaded with Uncle Lofton to stop there.

"No, we can't stop there," he said.

"Why can't we?"

"Because that's for white people."

I didn't understand.

"They don't want us in their places," he said.

After some hours of driving further, we arrived at the house in the mountains where my father "lived." We drove up a steep road and saw a large house with a big fence. There were many buildings, and everywhere white men with guns. The black men had on striped suits and striped hats.

As soon as she saw these men, my mother began to cry. Aunt Amanda said, "Oh, Jesus," and started to crying too. Me and my brother and Uncle Lofton and Uncle Jack were the only ones who didn't cry. But Uncle Lofton and Uncle Jack were very sad.

Uncle Lofton stopped the car, and a white man with a gun came to the car and talked to him. Then we got out of the car and followed him to a big gate with thick bars.

A big fat white man came up to Aunt Amanda.

"Your brother is too nice a person to be in here," he said. He told her we should follow him to where we could see him.

Uncle Lofton held our hands tightly. All the other black men in striped suits were coming up to me and Knee and saying how good we looked in our sailor suits.

After we were in the room for a few minutes, a door opened, and a man, a very dark man, came into the room and smiled at us. He was so glad to see us.

Everybody stood there just looking at him. He didn't have on a striped suit, but a gray one. Aunt Amanda was the first one to grab him and hug him tight. Then me and my brother. Then my mother went up to him and hugged him. Then Uncle Jack and then Uncle Lofton.

"How are you?" he said.

"Fine," my mother said. "Fine, and you okay?"

"Okay, they treat me okay."

"You look fine."

"Oh, don't he look fine," Aunt Amanda said.

"Thanks."

"We brought you some cake and chicken. They let you have that?"

"Oh, yeah."

"Here," Uncle Lofton said, giving him the cigarettes. "Something Buster Jacob told me to tell you," and he told him something in a mutter and he laughed.

"How is old Buster?" he asked.

"Oh, he's okay. They all okay."

He asked about Grand Papa, and they gave him the present from him. After they talked a while, I was allowed to tell him what Mr. Roy Melvin said about coming back to help him out with the coons. After a while, he kneeled down to me and my brother and held us to him for a long time. I could smell his clean, freshly pressed clothes.

He told the man he wanted to take us with him. The man who was white said it was alright. We went out into the yard and every time my father came to somebody, he would stop and tell them we were his sons. When we were alone, he sat me down on one knee and Knee on the other knee. I was afraid somebody had told him about my temper tantrum, but he didn't mention it.

"I want you boys to promise me something," he said.

"Okay," I said.

"Until I come and live with you again, I want you to promise that you will be good boys, okay?"

"We are good boys," I assured him.

"I want you, Morris, to take care of your little brother. Don't let anything bad happen to you! Do you understand?"

"Yessir!"

He said we should go to church and believe in God.

He pressed his head to my shoulder for a few minutes and cried. I felt so sad suddenly.

Okay, I said to myself, I'll promise to be good and I'll look out for my little brother. I'll be good, and love God, and say my prayers every night.

When we were saying good-bye to him, I didn't understand why he couldn't come with us.

"Uncle Lofton, why can't he come?"

"He can't come."

Knee grabbed my sleeve and said, "I don't like him. He's black!"

"Yes, but he's our father!" I whispered, already prepared to like him no matter what. I had a thousand questions to ask Uncle Lofton about my father, and I knew that he would do his best to tell me the truth.

On the way back, I looked out again at the mountains from the car window. They didn't bring me joy as they had when we drove past them that morning; now they filled me with dread.

Chapter 3

〜〜〜〜〜〜〜〜〜〜〜〜

"**M**anda," Uncle Lofton said, "what we gonna do about the other boy?"

The other boy was my little brother, whom I had not seen since we came back from the Shenandoah Valley. My mother took Cornelius with her to live at my grandmother's.

"Uncle Lofton, where is my real mamma?" I asked him, suddenly feeling I could ask him anything.

"She suppose to be living up there with her mother, your Grandma Commie."

"Are we going to see her?"

"Son, if she wants to see you, she knows where you are. Now you forget all about that now, alright. We got to go get yo brother."

"When is my mother coming back?" I asked.

"We don't know that," Uncle Lofton said.

"Nobody knows where Dorothy is," Amanda said. "What kind of mother is she to leave her children!"

"I think we ought to go up to Mrs. Commie's and get that boy!" Lofton said.

"Ain't nobody there to take care of that child!" Amanda grunted, "and these here is my brother's chilluns." She started out the door, pushing the back of my head into the direction of the car.

"We got one," Lofton agreed. "Let's get the other one."

I felt lonely in the backseat. When the car stopped, I saw a house with a bunch of people staring at us. Some were hanging out of the opened windows, others sat on the porch and the garden. As we approached, they laughed and joked out loud.

"Come here, Morris," one of the tall yellow boys called to me.

"Naw," I said, and twisted my elbow out of his easy grip.

"You done been up in the Shenandoah," he laughed. "Hell, you don't even recognize your own people!"

"That little nigger done got citified?" another boy laughed.

"Yeah, and he ain't but two years old."

"Put him on the dog's back," another one yelled. "See if he can ride him."

One of them grabbed me and put me on the back of a big dog that seemed as big as a horse. I was so frightened that I grabbed the collar of the dog to hold on.

"Look at im now! He think he somethin," one of the boys yelled.

"Nigger, is you on a horse!"

"Think he a cowboy!"

The dog seemed to like the idea of riding me around like a horse; he didn't try to throw me off but ambled along as if he had been riding little boys all his life.

The dog walked through the house with me on his back. The house smelled of sulphur and strange, pungent and exotic odors. He led me through the kitchen to the back porch, where I saw several more people lying in the sun. Chickens were pecking corn in the yard, and farther away were rows of corn and peas and cabbage. In the field several people were working.

"Take that boy off the dog," Uncle Lofton said. Taking me by the arm, he and Aunt Amanda started out to the field.

The sun was hot, but as we came into the cornfield, the wide green leaves threw a cooling shade across my head. We passed through to the pea patch. My aunt and uncle and I approached a woman who was squatting down on her knees picking peas. It wasn't until we were close to her that she looked up; it was then I saw the little brown baby asleep in the shade of a stalk of peas.

"Howdy, Mrs. Commie." They called my grandmother Commie. She didn't know what a commie was. She was, if anything, a conjure woman, a "root doctor," an evil woman who could work spells on people. Her real name was Connie Marie Dana Waddell, but everybody knew her as Mrs. Commie.

"How you doing, Mrs. Commie," Aunt Amanda said.

"I'm fair to middle," she replied.

"Mrs. Commie," Uncle Lofton said, coming to the point without batting an eye. "We come to get that child."

17

"Now, Lofton," she said in a high, squeaky voice, "you know these children is my daughter's children and I want to keep them here."

"You got too many mouths to feed as it is," Aunt Amanda said.

"Ain't nobody gonna starve in this family, Manda," Grandma Commie said.

"But Dorothy ain't gonna take care of these children," Uncle Lofton said. "She don't care nothing about these children."

"Don't make no difference, they hers."

"They hers," Amanda said, "but where is she now? My brother is up in the prison and he told me to see about his boys. Now, you know that Dorothy ain't got no mind to take care of these children!"

"What kind of woman is it that don't care about her children!" Uncle Lofton said.

Grandma Commie shot a brown bullet of snuff into the ground near a pea stalk.

"Now you lissen to me! Culphert"—Culphert was my father's name, but sometimes they called him Cuffy—"Culphert ought to know when he went to jail that Dorothy is a young woman."

"A young woman?" Uncle Lofton knew about the reputation of the Waddell women. He knew what everybody else had known about them. How these high-yeller women were loose. Everybody knew the story of their family, of Dana Hatcher, the woman who had three children by the white man at the plantation, the man who owned her mother, and everybody knew that she had turned right around and had three more by the blackest man she could find. Compensation, somebody said. He knew that Dana never bothered with conventional morality like marriage, that she boasted about her female attraction, and that she "lived on the same street as prostitutes but she wasn't one of them."

"Still a young woman?" my Aunt Amanda grunted disapprovingly. The boldness of the Waddell women always shocked her.

"That's right! Dorothy is still a young woman! You can't expect her to stay home with these children just because he is in jail!"

Before Grandma Commie could say another word, Uncle Lofton reached under the pea stalk and picked my baby brother up and wheeled and started back to the house.

Grandma Commie jumped up from her position and went after him and the baby.

18

"Lofton, you leave my daughter's children here! Leave that baby here!"

Uncle Lofton turned to her.

"This baby is filthy and shitty all over! What can you do with this child?"

"Well, leave Morris with us," Grandma Commie shouted.

"Morris, you come on," Aunt Amanda told me. I ran up to them and all the way to the house, afraid that one of my uncles would reach out and grab me and keep me with them.

Chapter 4

Aunt Amanda woke us up at the crack of dawn. "After we take Uncle Lofton to work, we goin to work ourselves," she said. After breakfast, we drove Uncle Lofton out to A. J. Harris's store, where other members of his section were waiting to go to work on the railroad.

I stood by and listened to Uncle Lofton and Mr. Roy Melvin greet each other. "Hey, Lofton, you up and stirring?" Mr. Roy Melvin asked. Mr. Roy Melvin wore a red bandana around his neck, a denim jacket and overalls, and big black hard-toe boots. We knew that his harmonica was in his pocket.

"I'm rearin to go!" Uncle Lofton said. "Mandy," he added, turning to Aunt Amanda, "what bout you?"

"I'm sprightly this morning, Roy," she said. "How you doin?"

"I'm right pert," he chuckled. "Never felt better and had so little!"

"Me and these boys goin over to Sam Dallason's and pick us some cotton," she told the men who sat in the shadows of the morning darkness.

They sat on the bench in front of the red brick store, waiting for Mr. Harris to come out of his brick house next door. They held their black lunch boxes beneath their arms, their long leather gloves in their hands, and wore their striped blue railroad caps tight on their heads.

The red and white Mobil gas tanks stood like two additional men.

"I hear you boys goin to pick some cotton," he laughed.

"Your goin to make you all some money. What you spect you goin do wit all that money, Morris?"

"I want to buy myself a car," I told him.

"A *ka-ah-r!*"

Since we had come back from visiting my father in prison, I had wanted a car, a convertible. I saw a young white boy driving a yellow convertible car in Wilmington. When I asked Uncle Lofton how old the boy was, he said he was about sixteen years old. I decided that I would be sixteen one day soon, and that I would need a convertible.

"I low it's goin take a lot of work to buy a car, ain't it?"

Oh, yes, I knew that, but I was a very fast cotton picker.

"Is you now? When did you start picking cotton?" Aunt Amanda asked. "I never knowed you to pick cotton fore now."

I had never picked cotton before, but I vowed to pick fast enough to buy myself a car in one day. Everybody laughed.

"All right, boys," Mr. Harris said, coming out of his brick house. "How's everybody today?" He was a squat man, with a reddish, flat face. He wore a red plaid jacket and black rubber boots.

"Top of the day to you, Mr. Harris," Uncle Lofton said, greeting the white man.

"Top of the morning to you," Mr. Roy Melvin said to him. The other men grunted their greetings and then got up.

"I want my driving men to listen up now," Mr. Harris said. "The section gang from Wilmington are not going to work their regular route today," he said, "so we're going to have do their part too."

"Them from Wilmington, they come down there as far as Acme?"

"That's right. Okay, let's go!"

They started walking across 74–76 to the railroad station across the tracks. My brother and I watched the group longingly as it faded into the morning mist. How exciting it was watching the railroad men work.

"Aunt Amanda," I asked, pulling on her skirt, "can we go watch them put the car on the tracks?"

"I reckon so," she said, as she looked at Mrs. Harris, a stout woman in a blue polka-dot dress, coming around the corner of the store.

"Good morning, Mandy," she said, as she opened the door to the store. "How you doin this morning?"

21

"Oh, I'm fair to middling," Aunt Amanda said, turning to us. "Now run over there and come right back when I call you. Watch and see if a car is coming fore you git in that road."

We were off like a shot. We paused at the highway and flew up to the tracks.

Just as we arrived, the men had rolled the steel section handcar out of the garage.

"Okay, boys, lift her up!" Mr. Harris commanded. The four men lifted the iron-wheeled cart onto the rails. They went back to the shed and picked up hammers, spikes, and iron bars and loaded them on the cart. Then they put their lunch boxes on the cart and climbed on. In the middle of the cart was a lever which was operated like a seesaw to make the cart go.

"Mr. Roy Melvin, where is the motor?" I called to them.

"We is the motor," he laughed back.

"Good-bye!" we called to them. Uncle Lofton smiled and waved to us. All the men waved except Mr. Harris. We watched them as they moved down the railroad, pumping up and down.

"Okay, boys," Mr. Harris said, as the car stopped. "Lineup men!" he called. A man with a long iron bar came forward. "Okay, line her up!" The men put the iron bar against the rail and pushed it until it was aligned to the place on the wooden track where the spike would go.

"Lean forward, lineup man, lean forward!" That meant the lineup man would push forward against the rail.

"Jack! Put a jack under her, boys!" The men scrambled to place a rail jack under the rail to raise it up.

"Drive her!" Mr. Harris shouted. I could barely make out the figure of the drivers, Mr. Roy Melvin and Uncle Lofton, as they lifted their hammers and hit the spikes, causing the rails to ring and vibrate all the way down the line.

"Drive her in, boys!"

Soon we heard Mr. Roy Melvin singing.

> "Railroad Man, ain't got no home! *Hah!*
> Here today, tomorrow gone—*Hah!*"

Every time Mr. Roy Melvin said "hah!" they swung their hammers down on the steel spike, singing.

> "Look who I see coming down the street! *Hah!*
> With a pretty dress on—*Hah*
> Must be somebody comin' to me!—*hah!*"

"Youuhooo!"

It was Aunt Amanda calling. We turned and made our way back across 74–76, past the sycamore tree and back to the store.

"What else can I get for you, Manda?" Mrs. Harris was saying as we came in.

"Oh, I guess you can get me two straw hats for my boys. They going to pick cotton with me this morning over at Sam Dallason's place."

"Is that a fact? These boys sho is little uns."

"They wants that money," Aunt Amanda said, glancing down at us. "Y'all wants money, don't you?"

Mrs. Harris took down two straw hats and handed them to us. They looked like the one cowboy Gabby Hayes wore. The string went up around the neck. Just like the cowboy's did.

"Now put that on my count," Aunt Amanda said.

"You betcha," Mrs. Harris said. As we left the store, she called out, "Now don't stay in the sun too long now, boys."

Aunt Amanda drove past the Gum Swamp graveyard, past our house, finally slowing down to turn down a long dirt road with a leaning mailbox. As we drove down this smooth dirt road, rows of tall white cotton waved to us from endless fields.

By the time Aunt Amanda pulled into the yard dominated by a gigantic tree weighted and dripping with gray river moss, I could hardly contain my excitement. I was going to pick cotton; I was going to buy that yellow convertible. I would drive it everywhere. I would not even wait until I was sixteen. I jumped out of the backseat just as a screen door opened in the middle of the long white porch. A fat white man, his hands under his barrellike belly, wobbled out of it.

"Good mornin, Manda!" he bellowed. "You bright and early! You up and mighty sprightly!"

"Mister Dallason," she said, "I'm pert, this morning. That's right. I feel like I cin pick a hundred pounds foe I eat my lunch."

He looked down at me and my brother. "Is these them boys?"

"Yais, that's them. My brother's boys."

"Cuffy's boys."

"That's right."

"Nice-looking chaps. You ain't tellin me they's going to pick cotton, too?"

"Oh yes they is."

He watched Aunt Amanda pull the croker sacks out of the back of the car.

"Now you come here, Morris."

She was going to make me a sack to put my cotton in. I knew this from having watched people pick cotton before. I had seen many black people with croker sacks.

"You ain't big enough for a big sack," Aunt Amanda said, and held up a small feed sack, about half the size of her croker sack.

My sack was made from burlap, which made me feel that I was being treated as a grown-up. She pulled the sack to my waist, measured it, and then ripped two holes in it with the hooked blade of a barlow knife, which she folded and slipped back into the bib of her overalls.

With a look of satisfaction on her face, she slipped a piece of rag through the holes and tied the ends in a knot.

"Heah," she said. "Slip yo noggin through this." I put my head through the loop, which I pulled down across my shoulder.

"Let your arms hang down natural," she said, "so I can see how high you sack should go." My arm hung high over the sack. The string was too long. Patiently, she untied the knot and pulled the sack closer to my shoulder.

"Now git in that field and pick me a hundred pounds of cotton!"

I ran proudly to the cotton field that grew close up to the house, hearing the laughter of Mr. Sam Dallason and Aunt Amanda behind me.

Reaching the first cotton stalk, I plunged my fingers into the big white cushion and yanked at it. The cotton yielded easily. Opening my sack, I threw it inside and watched it float slowly down and rest behind a fold. How many times would I have to do this before the cotton would be at the top?

"Now that boy ain't lazy," Sam Dallason called out. "No sir, he ain't!"

"I ain't lazy, either!" Knee shouted impatiently. Aunt Amanda was putting the loop over his head.

"Now git in that field and pick me a hundred pounds!" She consecrated him, and he shot out of her arms toward the field and me. He fell once but picked himself up and, grabbing the end of the sack like a girl picking up the end of a long dress, started running again.

When he had picked his first boll of cotton, Aunt Amanda and

Sam Dallason clapped, whooped, and hollered, just like they had done with me.

"Aunt Manda," I yelled to her. "Come on and pick cotton too!"

She said she was coming and then told Mr. Sam Dallason that she hoped Mrs. Sam Dallason wasn't feeling so puny and that she hoped she got better soon so that she could help them pick some of this cotton. Mr. Sam Dallason said he was sure his wife would be feeling a whole lot better and he would tell her Mandy had asked about her, but that his wife was not cut out for working in the fields. He went back into the big white screened porch and Aunt Amanda, tying her sack around her waist, came out to the field.

"Now, boys," she said, "here's how you pick cotton. Don't worry about these green ones, they ain't open yet. When they ain't open, the cotton is not ready. Just take the ones that open like that. See here these ones that's closed, open them first, but be careful because of these sticky thorns. Be careful, they will cut your fingers around the fingertips . . ."

While Aunt Amanda talked, her black hands attacked the soft white cotton with such rapidity that I thought of Uncle Lofton's chickens pecking corn that Uncle Lofton would throw at them. Just as the chickens' heads darted everywhere, her hands moved amazingly fast all over the cotton stalk. They went from the top to the bottom, from the side to way over in the back of the stalk, and then down on the ground to retrieve a fallen boll.

"There's a wrong way to pick cotton, and there's a right way," she said, "just like anything else . . . and if you do it the right way, you save yourself time and money."

She worked a row with me on the right and my brother on the left. When she had picked her row up a short distance, she would turn and pick back on Knee's row; reaching us, she would go back up on my row.

"I'm gonna help you boys out," she said. Seeing my brother play at a boll, she told him to leave it alone. It was green and had not blossomed yet.

After a while, Knee said he was tired of picking cotton.

"I thought you boys was wanting to make some money?" she asked us.

"But why do we have to pick cotton?" he wanted to know.

"To get money."

"But why do we need money?"

"We got to eat, don't we?"

"Don't we need money to buy school clothes and stuff like that?" I asked her.

"You don't start school until two weeks."

"Is that a long time?"

"Long enough for you to make enough money to buy you something for school."

"And can I buy a lunch box with Hoopla Long Cassidy on it?"

"Depends on how much cotton you pick."

"I'll pick a lot!"

"And don't you want some money to buy something to send you daddy?"

We did, I told her. At least I did.

"What else you want to buy? You want to buy something for your mother?"

I didn't know about that. "I'm going to buy a car and drive it."

"Ouch!" My fingers stuck into the thorn of a cotton boll. The needle-size thorn pierced between the nail and the skin. As I screamed, Aunt Amanda grabbed my finger, kissed it, and said it was alright.

Aunt Amanda straightened up and looked over the field. "Where's he at?"

I looked for Knee and didn't see him. Then I crossed through the stalks and saw his straw hat. Next to his straw hat lay his sack, and lying on top of his sack, between two stalks, was my brother, fast asleep. A few cockleburs had wound themselves in his hair.

"Lord a mercy!" Aunt Amanda laughed. "Ain't that something. Done fall asleep!" The sound of a wagon directed our gaze to the road. The wagon was coming up the road with a bunch of black people.

"Here they come," Aunt Amanda said, waving to the truck. "Hey! Whooeee! Ha, ha, ha! You-hooo!" She looked down at me.

"They late. To make any money in this world, boy, you got to get up early in the morning!" I laughed with her. "See, I've done made me a couple dollars already and they just getting here."

The wagon stopped, discharging its riders, mostly women, onto the field. As they came closer, I saw that they were Mrs. Suzanne, Mr. Roy Melvin's wife, and her twins.

26

"Mandy, how much yo done picked?" Mrs. Suzanne asked excitedly. When she saw Aunt Amanda's sack, she screeched, and said, "Lawd have mercy!"

With a clap of laughter, the others began picking cotton, bowing their heads down like they were saying their prayers. All the while they worked, they were lallygagging.

"Manda, I want you to bake me two mo them apple pies!"

"Oh, wasn't them pies good, Suzanne?"

"Oh, Manda, honey, my children ate them two pies; I just got a skimption for myself. What you put in them pies that make em so good?"

"Well, I'll tell you . . ."

They were working but they sounded like they were playing a game. And their hands! After pulling a cocklebur out of my hair, I pillowed my head down on the row to peep up from the stalks, where I could see their disembodied hands, which leaped over the stalks with a life of their own.

While I was looking at their hands, an insect crawled across the stalk. I asked Aunt Amanda what it was. She said it was a boll weevil which would destroy the cotton. I decided to collect the weevils in a jar and present them to Mr. Sam Dallason. How much would he give me for a jar full of them?

"I don't know," she said, "but it seems like you and your brother don't want to pick this cotton. So why don't you and Knee go get us some water. You can be the waterjacks."

"Can we be waterjacks?" I asked, liking the idea immediately. The sun had risen now, and it was getting hot. As I looked across the cotton field, small heat waves began to rise.

"Look at them sun devils!" Mrs. Suzanne said.

"We need some water," Aunt Amanda said again, turning to me. "Go to the car, get that jar and pump some fresh water and bring it to us."

"Okay."

"And don't be making a lot of noise, cause Mrs. Sam Dallason is feeling puny day. She sickly. And don't you stop and mess with that man's pear trees."

Knee and I tore off for the car to get the jar. As we came up the back of Sam Dallason's house, we passed his pigpen, the turkeys, the guinea hens, and then the pear tree. The pear tree was loaded down with big, ripened, yellow pears.

Knee picked one up and started to bite it.

"No! We shouldn't mess with that old white man's pears!" I admonished him. Sadly, he put the pear down. Oh, how I wanted to eat one of them myself!

"If we eat them," I told him, "something bad might happen to us."

"Like what?"

I thought of our father in prison. Maybe he was there because he had done something bad like steal somebody's pears.

"I don't know."

Then another thought occurred to me. Maybe they have an idiot in their house. Kenny Melvin had told me that white people often kept idiots in their houses.

We approached the back of the big white house. How did the white people live? What did they have in their house? What room did they have their idiot in? A monster that would chase you and eat you if it caught you? If I looked into the window, nobody would know it. I eased up to the house and pulled myself up. But before I could look, I saw a white woman. She was lying on the porch sleeping in a swing. She didn't see us, but seeing her was enough to discourage me from looking into the window.

Hurrying to the car, we got the jar and retraced our way back and saw that she had not moved.

When we came to the pear tree again, I asked my brother if he felt like eating a pear. My father in prison had told me that I was to be good. I could be good and not eat a pear, but couldn't my brother eat a pear?

So I gave him one to eat.

He bit so deeply into the soft fruit that the juices ran down the corner of his mouth. I couldn't just stand there and let him eat a pear and not taste one myself, so I ate one too. We ate pears until we couldn't eat any more, loving the juicy, soft, sweet taste, and filling our pockets with them.

Just as we were walking back, I saw a male turkey. A gobbler! He was about three feet high, but he seemed the size of an elephant. We had done something bad, and now he was going to get us for it.

The gobbler spread his purple, yellow, blue, and black tail feathers threateningly. His brown wings unfolded, exposing white skin and blowing dried leaves around on the ground like a tornado; he thrust his head right into my face. I gazed into his red snout, staring at the red jowl which hung down his heaving puffed chest like a necktie of flowing blood.

As we stood there, frozen in panic, the gobbler emitted a deafening guttural noise like the cry of attacking Indians.

"Oh, Mister Turkey!" Knee pleaded, "we won't eat your pears no more!"

The turkey moved closer to us, spreading its tail feathers wider. I turned and ran, almost knocking Knee down. Thinking that he had been hit by the turkey, Knee screamed.

We ran so fast that we forgot the water jar which had slipped to the ground and spilled.

When we cut across the field, we were screaming as loud as we could. Aunt Amanda and the others looked up and saw us running and the turkey running behind us. When we got to her, she was laughing. I looked behind me for the first time to see if the turkey was still there.

"I told you bout meddling with other people's things," she said, pulling the pears from my pockets.

"Boy, is you stealing that man's pears?" Dorothy Mae, one of the cotton pickers, asked me.

Mr. Dallason suddenly appeared in front of me. He was so close that I could see his wrinkled white features under the straw hat; I could also see where the straw hat didn't protect his red neck. The wrinkled skin on his neck and jowl was as red as the skin on the gobbler's snout and jowl. This bloody red skin frightened me, and I wanted to scream.

"Put the pears behind you!" Dorothy Mae whispered to me.

"No," I said, "I ain't stealing them!" Stealing I knew was bad. Was stealing what my father did? Was he so tempted by pears that he stole some as I had done and gone to jail? I watched Mr. Sam Dallason's big, red, beefy face. "I'm eating them!"

He laughed.

"No, he's an honest boy," he said. "Eat all the pears you want." His teasing voice relieved me of my fear of being scolded. "But don't steal them!"

My brother and I sat quietly, still trembling from the encounter with the turkey as the men weighed our cotton for the day. A rope had been thrown over a tree limb, and a big black weight had been attached to it. A young black man was holding a large sack of cotton under the scale while another one hooked the sack to it.

Aunt Amanda had placed a big handful of cotton in Knee's sack and then a big handful in my sack. She did this without anybody else seeing her. She winked at me when I saw her doing it.

After the cotton was weighed, Mr. Sam Dallason went back up to the big house, and we ate the lunch Aunt Amanda brought us. We sat under the shade tree in a cow-stomp and the women lallygagged some more and me and my brother played, trying to collect some more boll weevils.

"Alright," Aunt Amanda said to the others, "let's go now." They all got their sacks and went back in the field. As we came along beside the house, I saw Mr. Sam Dallason sleeping on a chair.

"Why don't Mr. Dallason ever pick cotton?" I asked Aunt Amanda.

"He's a white man," she said, and Mrs. Suzanne laughed out loud.

"He sho is that," she said.

"White people don't ever pick cotton?"

"But I tell you one thing," Aunt Amanda said to Mrs. Suzanne, "I don't begredge these white people nothin. They got they problem. Look at his puny wife."

"Uh-huh!" Mrs. Suzanne said, "and look at how lazy all his chillum is."

The sun was so hot that it made me sleepy. I slept under the coolness of a cotton stalk. When I woke up, Aunt Amanda was standing over me laughing.

"Boy, you know we got to go get Lofton now!" She looked at her shadow on the ground. "It's almost four o'clock!"

I got up and looked around. All the people were looking at me. Mr. Sam Dallason was handing me some money.

"You boys picked a lot of cotton today," he said.

On the way to pick Uncle Lofton up from work, my brother and I talked about the money we made picking cotton. Aunt Amanda laughed with us, teasing us about the turkey.

When we came to the railroad, we could see the men still working and hear them singing. As they sang, Mr. A. J. Harris would tell them what to do. Some of the men hammered the steel spikes into the crossties, while others hauled the long black crossties up from the railroad cart. When they had the cart loaded with crossties, they pumped a lever to make the cart slide down the rail to where Uncle Lofton worked. There they unloaded another crosstie under the rail. Mr. Roy Melvin placed the spike on the crosstie, and Uncle Lofton hammered it.

"Uhhhh—ha!" Uncle Lofton yelled as he brought the big hammer down on the spike.

"Alright, boys," Mr. Harris shouted, standing a safe distance away, his hands on his hips. "Come on, boys!"

Uncle Lofton swung the hammer again.

"Hunhh!" he yelled as the hammer sailed over his head.

After a while, Mr. Harris, pulling out his pocket watch and looking at it, said, "Okay, boys, let's knock for today. That's it, boys."

Uncle Lofton and Mr. Roy Melvin walked in our direction. Uncle Lofton handed his lunch box to me as he got in the car behind the wheel. Mr. Roy Melvin got in the back with us. As he and Uncle Lofton talked with Aunt Amanda, Knee and I opened the lunch box to see if he had left something for us. We found he hadn't eaten the biscuit. I ate a bite and gave my brother a bite. It was more delicious than a whole meal. It had a smell like it had been saved just for us. Sometimes he would even leave a whole slice of pie.

When Mr. Roy Melvin teased us about the turkey incident, I asked him, mainly to distract him, if he sang songs on the railroad.

"I be singing them songs and the boys be lining themn spikes up! Yeah, I be the one that's singing."

"How much money you make?"

"We average about a dollar and a half a day! Thirty dollars a month. Ain't that right, Lofton?"

"That's bout right," Uncle Lofton said.

"How much do Mr. Harris make?"

"Mr. Harris? Now why you want to know that?"

"Well, how much does he make?"

"Mr. Harris? Now, he gits the boss man price."

"What's the boss man price?"

"Bout thirty dollars a day!"

"Is that a lot?"

"Heh, heh! Yeah, that is plenty money."

"Sure it is," Uncle Lofton said.

"Man, shucks, that lil ol bit we gets is a lot of money! Yeah, buddy. Things is tough. I have worked for twenty cents a day, Morris!"

"That's right, Morris," Uncle Lofton said. "I use to work for twenty-five cents a day too. Roy is telling the truth!"

"And then I got a raise to seventy-five cents! Oh, I had plenty money then!"

31

CECIL BROWN

"But I made twenty-five cents today!"

"Things is getting better," Mr. Roy Melvin said. "I used to work all day in a white man's field for a quarter and be happy that I could get that quarter. Now look at you. Done made two quarters and you ain't even start school yit!"

When we were home, Mr. Roy Melvin said good-bye and started across the plank that led to the path to his house.

"Mr. Roy, can you tell us a story about Mr. Rabbit?"

"Naw, not now, Morris," he said. "Ain't you going to help Lofton with the bacco?"

"After you help me with the bacco barn, maybe you can go over and play with Roy's children."

I followed Uncle Lofton and Aunt Amanda down to the tobacco barn.

Uncle Lofton opened the barn door. The heat, mixed with the pungent sweet smell of curing tobacco, rushed over my face. Uncle Lofton felt the leaves of the tobacco.

"One more day," he muttered to Aunt Amanda.

"Well, we'll be taking it to the market in Whiteville," Aunt Amanda said. "Day after tomorrow!"

We walked back to the house. Aunt Amanda went into one of the rooms where they had stored tobacco.

"I'm going to grade for a hour, Lofton," she said, and she sat down between two piles of tobacco and started sorting it out into three grades.

"Come on and help me feed up now, boys," Uncle Lofton said, and we followed him out the back of the house to the shed. He threw some hay to the white mare, mixed swill for the hogs and put it in their pen, then he shelled corn for the chicken and ducks. He milked the cow and gave the milk to us to carry to the house.

When we got into the house with the milk, Aunt Amanda was taking the biscuits out of the oven.

"Can we go over to Mr. Roy Melvin's?" I asked her.

"Go on over there, but be back. But I'm gonna holler for you now when we ready to eat."

The footpath to Mr. Roy's started out as pleasant, well-worn, and sunny as it passed through Uncle Lofton's cornfield, but then it came to a hedge of trees that cast somber, foreboding shadows. Past the trees, the path turned even more somber, for it seemed that all the light had been squeezed out of the sky by the tall pine trees until there was total darkness.

32

In the middle of this dark loom was a deep pond. This pond held many mysteries and powers. It was inhabited by demons, spirits, hants, and the most frightening of all southern monsters, the "boogeyman." Sometimes, with a rain, it could measure up to a man's waist and could swallow a child. To get past the pond, you had to walk on either side of the path.

When we came into the yard, Mr. Roy Melvin was sitting on the steps with his children playing his harp. Mr. Roy Melvin and his wife Suzanne and their children were poor. I always liked that they were poorer than we were. Poverty meant that there were so many children to play with.

Aunt Amanda said they were poor because Mr. Roy Melvin threw away his money on other women, and that was why Kenneth and Booty and their sisters went to school in rags. But Uncle Lofton said Mr. Roy Melvin didn't throw his money away on women, but that the reason they were so poor was that they had so many children.

"Tell us a story, Mr. Roy," I asked him.

"It all had to do with Brother Rabbit," he said.

"Brother Rabbit?"

"Yeah, Brother Rabbit was mad."

"What was he mad about?"

"He was mad because Brother Fox had two beautiful daughters and both of them liked Brother Wolf."

We all gathered around Mr. Roy to hear the story.

"Square off and let these old bones sit down here," Mrs. Suzanne said, coming out of the house. "I likes to hear a good story about the Brother Rabbit too."

I was hoping Aunt Amanda wouldn't call us to come eat just when Mr. Roy Melvin was getting in the middle of telling us about Brother Rabbit.

"This was a dilemma for Brother Rabbit," Mr. Roy Melvin said. "But Brother Rabbit don't care nothing bout no dilemmas."

"He sho don't," Mrs. Suzanne said.

"So he had to start some trickaration," Mr. Roy went on. "So this is how he did it.

"When Brother Fox told Brother Rabbit that somebody had been going into his corn patch and messing with his corn, Brother Rabbit thought he would blame it on Brother Wolf. Naturally, it was Brother Rabbit messin in that corn patch! So he said to Brother Fox, 'Don't worry, I know who's been in your field.' Fox said, 'You do? Who?' Said Brother Rabbit, 'I won't tell you who, but I'll bring him to your daughters' party and let *him* tell *you* to *your face!*'

"The fox's daughters were having this party. They was real good-looking gals, too. So Brother Rabbit went to Brother Wolf and said, 'You going to the party?' Brother Wolf said, 'Yeah!' Brother Rabbit said, 'But are you going to sing too?' 'Sing?' asked Brother Wolf. 'Yeah, sing. There's going to be a lot of singing at this party. I'm going to sing. Why don't you sing with me? You got a good bassing voice. Man, you can really bass.' He was sweet-talkin' the Wolf, see? Getting on his good side, to get him into some devilment. Brother Wolf wanted to be in with Brother Rabbit so he said he would knock around with him on bass. So they practiced a little bit. Brother Rabbit said, 'Look here, man, here's what we goin' do: whenever I sing, "Who was in my cornfield," you sing, "Nobody but me." ' Brother Wolf axed him, said, 'Is that all?' Brother Rabbit said, 'Yah, that's all. Get it?' He made Brother Wolf repeat it. Brother Wolf wasn't too bright. He said to himself, 'No matter what you say, all I sing is "Nobody but me." Okay, I got it.'

"So they went to the party. In the middle of the party, Brother Rabbit told them he had a special song to sing. He started singing, 'Who was in Brother Fox's cornfield?' Brother Wolf started really bassing, 'Nobody but me, nobody but me!' "

Mr. Roy sung *"Nobody but me!"* in a deep voice that sounded like Nat King Cole.

Before he started playing the harp again, Mr. Roy said, "Hey, boys, let's go!"

That was our signal to dance. First, me and my brother started dancing. Then his own children, Kenny, Booty, Annie, and Malsie, jumped in. Mrs. Suzanne started laughing. We danced and Mr. Roy Melvin played.

"Ain't nobody but me!"

We danced and sang for a long time, and when it was finished it made me feel proud to see how much Mr. Roy Melvin liked us.

"Ain't nobody but me!"

When he was exhausted, he stopped, put his harp down, and finished the story.

"Brother Fox heard that and started beating Brother Wolf's butt. *'You the one in my cornfield!'* He started yelling, *'No, it wasn't me!' 'Yes it was, you said it right to my face!'* "

We laughed at Brother Wolf's unmasking.

"What happened to him then?" I asked.

"Oh, after that, he just flew off."

"How?"

"See, now back in them days," Mr. Roy said. "Back then, people had a good time. People could fly. Colored people could fly. That's right. A white man would be working some colored man to death, and the colored man would get tired of it, and just fly off."

"Ya—hoooo!"

Aunt Amanda's melodic cry reached through the hollow and echoed.

"That's Manda," Mr. Roy said. "Morris, you and Knee gots to go eat now."

I wanted to eat at their house. For dinner, Mrs. Suzanne would put out plates of molasses and flapjacks. I watched the other children to see how they ate it. Mrs. Suzanne would then put a piece of fatback on each plate. The children would clap and show a great deal of enthusiasm. But I knew, as I watched them, that I could eat better food than they did. At our house, we had piles of bologna, sausages, and mayonnaise and white bread.

"Okay, good-bye!" we yelled to them and turned back to the footpath and made our way home. Some of Mr. Roy's friends were coming up the other path to visit him.

As we headed down the footpath, I turned to see Mr. Roy in the middle of a group of clapping men, singing and blowing his harp. They were playing the blues. Some of the people I had seen before on Buster Jacob's porch had come up to visit and were now dancing to Mr. Roy's music.

Aunt Amanda and Uncle Lofton were waiting for us at the dinner table, along with Aunt Amanda's youngest brother, Elmo.

"Well, let me get my apern," Aunt Amanda said, "and go to the Anchorage Club." She worked for some white people at Lake Waccamaw.

After Aunt Amanda left, Uncle Lofton told us to go to bed and to remember to say our prayers. I kneeled by the bed and folded my hands, and prayed that if I should die before I wake, that the lord my soul would take.

"Now say the Lord's Prayer," Uncle Lofton said. He was lying in his own bed, talking to us through the wall, as he always did.

Just as I was going to sleep, I saw a monster in the bed. It was the turkey. It couldn't be my brother because he was sleeping at the other end of the bed. The turkey was coming back to get me because I had done something bad. Like my father, I had done something so bad, I was going to be punished.

"Uncle Lofton! The turkey is here!"

"There ain't no turkey in that bed!" he shouted back.

"Yes it is! I can see him!"

"He is too, Uncle Lofton!" my brother screamed.

Uncle Lofton got up out of bed and switched on the electric light.

"See, there's no turkey," he said, pointing to the pillow. "That's just a pillow. When I cut out the lights and"—he switched out the lights—"the moonlight makes a shadow, it just looks like a turkey."

We saw that he was right and felt relieved. Uncle Lofton put his arms around me and my brother and comforted us. It was at this moment that I began to associate my uncle with any security that I was to experience in the world, and to associate my father with the fear of doing something bad. It was at this time we began to call Uncle Lofton "Daddy."

Chapter 5

~~~~~~

"Look how red this land is," Uncle Lofton said.

Outside the land was bright orange. It had rained, and the red soil ran down the ditches in gushes. We were on our way to Aunt Gertie, another of my father's sisters, who lived in Clarkton, a small farming village about twenty miles from Bolton. Uncle Lofton and Aunt Amanda visited my father in prison as often as they could, which was two or three times a year. They would not always take me and my brother along because sometimes children were not allowed to visit. They would take along some of the adult relatives with them and leave my brother and me in the care of Aunt Gertie's oldest daughter, Selina.

Aunt Gertrude had four children, Selina, Linda, Flossie Belle, and Eli. Her husband had recently died in the hospital of TB.

While they prepared for the trip to see my father in prison, we were told to go outside and play. Flossie Belle and Eli came running up to us.

Flossie Belle wanted to play hide-and-go-seek. She was a tall black girl, about my age, with a moon face. She had a head full of pigtails with red, blue, and yellow rags tied to them and ran barefooted about in a raggedy frock.

Eli, my brother's age, who was very black, like all of them, wore raggedy short pants and a rag for a shirt. When I saw he didn't have shoes on, I was reluctant to play with him. Aunt Amanda and Uncle Lofton bought new clothes and shoes for us regularly, and this made me feel somehow better than my cousins.

"Do you know any riddles?" Eli asked me.

No, I didn't know any riddles. Besides, what was a riddle?

"What goes around the house but never goes in?"

I didn't know.

"A *path!*" I laughed. It was certainly the funniest joke I'd ever heard. I couldn't wait to tell it to somebody else.

"Mississippi is a hard word. I bet you can't spell it?"

I laughed again, then turned to see my cousins laughing at my stupidity. Mississippi was certainly a hard word for me to spell, but I was willing to try it. But before I could fix my mouth to say the first letter, he blurted out, "*I—T* spells it!"

I was astonished by his brilliance.

"What kind of flower is between yo nose and yo chin?"

While I was thinking about that, he said, "*Two-lips!*"

Flossie Belle and the rest of my cousins laughed at my stupidity. "Why does the chimney smoke?" Eli asked again.

"Because—"

"Because it can't *chew!*" he cackled and fell into a laughing frenzy as I stood helplessly looking at him. Did he think I was so stupid? Did the rest of them think I had never heard a riddle? Did they think they could laugh at us, dressed like they were!

I went up close to Eli and glared into his big shiny black eyes, grinning face, and threw back my fist and hit him as hard as I could. When he turned his face to cover his eye, I jumped on his back and bit him on the neck. He screamed, and I hit him on the head, first with my right and then my left fist.

"They fightin!" Flossie Belle screamed, running into the house.

Aunt Gertie appeared on the porch, with Uncle Lofton standing beside her.

"Cut that out, boy!" Uncle Lofton yelled. I drew back my fist and hit Eli again.

Uncle Lofton rushed over and pulled me off Eli. "What did you hit that boy for?" he yelled, shaking me with his strong arms. "Why did you hit your cousin?"

"Because he is so *ugly!!*" I said.

"You can't hit your own cousin like that!" Uncle Lofton demanded.

He brought me into the house. Aunt Gertie wiped the blood from Eli's face and held him close to her breast.

"Boy, don't you ever let me see yo come close to my child again!" She looked at Uncle Lofton. "What's wrong with him, Lofton? I thought you said he was well behaved."

"Boy, why did you do that?" Aunt Amanda asked me.

"Cause he so ugly," I said.

Aunt Amanda grunted.

"That child is goin go end up just like his daddy!" Aunt Gertie said. "Just like Culphert! You wait and see!"

Aunt Gertie was so angry that she refused to go with them to visit my father until Uncle Lofton had talked to me.

Why was there such a fuss over this, I wondered as Uncle Lofton pulled me aside. Fighting was nothing new to me and my brother. Didn't we break out the window in the car with our fighting? Even when we would fight in our new suits after Sunday school in the grass, Aunt Amanda and Uncle Lofton never got this mad.

"That was bad, Morris. You can't hit yo own cousin cause he is ugly," Uncle Lofton told me.

"Why can't I hit him?" I asked.

"You can't hit him for no reason. He yo cousin, boy. Don't you know what a cousin is? You got to know what a cousin is. Don't you know yet that you ain't suppose to hit your cousins? Answer me."

"I don't know."

"You don't know? You mean to tell me you don't know that? Don't be stupid, boy. Don't you know that cousins is the children that come from your mamma's sisters and brothers and from your daddy's sisters and brothers? Don't you even know that your Aunt Gertie's children is all your cousins? Flossie Belle and Eli and all the rest of them? And Uncle Jack's children? And Aunt Adelia's children? And Aunt Eunice's children Oscar Lee and Doris? And Aunt Johnnie Mae's children, Booker T . . . ?"

Were all black children in the world my cousins?

"Is Kenny and Willie our cousins?"

"No, they ain't no kin to you."

"Uncle Lofton, why did Aunt Gertie say I was going to be just like my daddy when I grow up?"

"What Gertie said that about you, Morris, that hurt my feelings," Uncle Lofton said.

"Why, Uncle Lofton? What did he do? Did he hit somebody?" I thought my father was like me. He would hit you if you were as ugly as cousin Eli.

"You are too young to know what he did. But when you get older, I'll tell you."

"When will he come back?"

"Oh, it's gonna be a while before your daddy come back. Forget that, son, you ain't gonna grow up like that. You just ain't. Not if I have anything to do with it."

I could see that he was hurt, but I didn't understand why. When I did understand it, I told myself, I would never forget what it was, because I didn't want to see Uncle Lofton hurting. I didn't want to do anything to make him mad with me.

"You getting to be a big boy," he said. "You have to grow up."

He looked worried, so I wanted to reassure him immediately that we enjoyed living with him and Aunt Amanda.

"I'm happy," I said and squeezed his hand. My brother dangled on the other side.

"You're happy." He laughed.

"Uh-huh!"

"Me, too!" Knee said.

"Well, it's time to leave you now," Uncle Lofton said. "You boys be good now and obey Selina."

They started for the car.

"Okay," I said, "I will be good."

We watched the car pull off and started back to the house and found Selina standing in the doorway.

"Now I am going to scrub and polish these floors," she said, "and I don't want none of you tracking up my flo! Do y'all understand?" Then she gave me another look. "Boy, you just as evil as Cuffy Brown, and if you think you gonna run over me or hit my brother, I'll beat the livin shit outa you. Do you understand me?"

"Yes," I nodded, suddenly afraid she would attack me. I took my brother's hand and led him off to a part of the yard. After a while Flossie Belle came over to us.

"Come on," she said, sticking her hand out for me to hold. "She crazy! We ain't study no flo. We can play with my shuck doll."

She pulled out her shuck doll and showed it to us. Flossie had taken an ear of corn and pulled the shuck off it, being careful to leave the silk tassel in place. The silk tassel became the doll's blond hair, which she combed and plaited. For a face she shelled off enough corn to paint in eyes, a nose, and a mouth. She had dressed the shuck doll in clothes she had made for her.

"Do you want to comb her hair?" Cousin Flossie asked me.

"Yeah!"

She handed the shuck doll and a tiny toy comb to me. I combed her hair gently.

As we were playing with Flossie's toy, we heard a shriek from the house and turned and saw Selina dashing from the porch after her sister Linda.

"Girl, I'm going to get yo ass!" Selina was screaming. Linda had tracked her floor but managed to escape by dashing into the cornfield.

"Don't pay them any mind," Flossie said. "Do you like wine?"

"Wine?" I had never heard about wine, but I was curious. We went up to the barn where Aunt Gertie made wine. Cousin Flossie took a tube from a barrel and showed us how to suck from it. I took a swig and it was only a short while before I was drunk. And the next thing I knew I was reeling from the barn, staggering and laughing to myself.

As I approached the back of the house, I saw Linda pull her dress up and squat down and piss in a beer bottle. I wondered what she was going to do with a beer bottle of piss. She called out to her sister Selina, "Selina, look what I found?"

Selina appeared in the doorway. My hatred for her returned.

"What chu got, girl?" she demanded of Linda.

Linda held up the beer bottle.

"I found a bottle of Mamma's beer!"

"Gimme that beer," Selina demanded and ran off the porch. Linda struggled with her long enough to effectively pull the trick off, and then finally let her have the beer. She then ran off a small piece to watch her drink it. I felt the urge to tell her that it was a trick, but then I was curious to see what Selina would do.

Selina put the bottle to her lips and was about to take a swig when Linda yelled out, "That's my *piss*, girl!" Selina threw the bottle down and shot off after Linda, who had cut a path through the cornfield. They ran to the end of the field where Selina finally caught up with her and, pulling a switch from a tree, beat her until she cried for mercy.

The whole day my cousins played tricks on each other, beat each other, and cried revenge. I identified with Linda, who was constantly playing tricks on her dominating sister Selina, a dictator of the first order. Everybody was afraid of her, even me.

That night Selina put supper on the back porch, since we were not allowed into the house until bedtime. But once we were in the

41

bedroom, we had to sleep on the floor on pallets. The playing continued until Selina finally had enough.

"Now if you chillun don't go to sleep, I'm gonna tell the Ku Klux Klan to come and get you?"

"The Ku Klux Klan? Who is that?" I asked.

"Thems white mens that will come and get you?" Selina told me. "They wear white sheets and they will get you." She went on to explain that they would burn a cross in the yard and when they did that, they were sure to get us.

"Look out the window!" Eli said. We rushed to the window and saw a cross burning in the yard.

"They coming after us!" Knee screamed and dashed for cover. I became frightened too.

"Look," Flossie said, and pointed to something that had escaped my attention. A Ku Klux Klanner in a white sheet was coming into the yard.

"Get the gun!" I screamed. Aunt Gertie kept her shotgun across the front door frame. "Get the gun!"

Flossie put a chair up to the door and got the gun down.

"Where's the shells?" Eli demanded.

"We can't find them!" Flossie replied.

"Oh, they gonna get us!" Knee cried. I looked around for Linda and Selina, but they were conspicuously absent. Where were they? Had the Ku Klux Klan got them already? I wished my real daddy was here, because I knew that he was bad and he wouldn't let the Klux Klan get us.

"I want my daddy! I want my daddy!" I started crying.

"Boy, yo better shut up and get in that bed!" Selina said, suddenly coming in the door. I was surprised to see her again and a bit relieved.

"The Ku Klux Klan said that if they come back and you boys ain't in bed they gonna get you for sho nough this time!"

We dove for the pallets and covered ourselves up and closed our eyes.

The next thing I remember was being taken from the floor by the gentle arms of Uncle Lofton and placed in the backseat of the car and being driven home to our beds back in Bolton.

Chapter 6

~~~~~~

The summers in Bolton were hot, and my brother and I watched as the black people worked in the fields cropping the tobacco, stringing it on sticks, and placing it in the barn, where it was cured. Then we watched Aunt Amanda and her friends Laura Melvin, Mary Bowen, and Mrs. Suzanne grade it. Then came the time to take it to Whiteville to the tobacco market. We were told that after we sold the tobacco, we would buy clothes for my first day at school which, Aunt Amanda assured me, was rapidly approaching.

Arriving in Whiteville, we approached the warehouse where many people were running up and down as if running away from somebody. I saw a lot of black people dressed up in Sunday clothes, but I didn't see any churches. There was a man without legs pushing himself along on a skateboard, rattling a tin cup, begging for money with sad eyes. His normal-looking face seemed juxtaposed with the severity of his deformity. Across the street, five black men in overalls were bending down on the sidewalk throwing a small cube against the wall. Every time the cube boomeranged against the wall, the men jumped up, cussed, yelled, and then threw their money into a pile which another man grabbed and put in his pocket, laughing at the others. When we asked Uncle Lofton what kind of game they were playing, he said we didn't need to know.

At the gate of the warehouse, a drunk Negro came to the window and offered all of us, my brother and me included, a drink from his bottle. Aunt Amanda grunted, and Uncle Lofton told him to go away. Behind him, a black woman dressed in a tight yellow skirt called him, and the man crossed the street, staggering and holding his bottle high over his head.

When we got inside the huge warehouse, I heard the loud talking of men everywhere and saw them laughing and slapping each other on the back. Everywhere white men were shaking hands with black men and exchanging money and smiling. Uncle Lofton and Aunt Amanda took their tobacco from the truck and stacked it in a line near a white man's tobacco.

Felton Bowen came up to us. He wanted to go get a soda and Uncle Lofton let me and Knee go with him. On our way, we passed a lot of black people sitting in front of a beautiful yellow convertible car. It was the same kind of car I had seen a young white boy drive and the kind I wanted for myself. A black man was leaning against it. He was a tall, good-looking man. He was wearing nice clothes and when he moved his hand, something shiny reflected in the sun. When he laughed, he threw his head back and laughed up to the sky.

I stopped and stared at him.

"Come on, Morris!" Felton yelled at us. But the man had seen me staring at him and he turned to me.

"Say, boy, what's you name?"

"Morris."

He laughed again.

Felton spoke up then. "That's Cuffy Brown's boys."

The man's expression changed. "Cuffy Brown? Is that Cuffy Brown's boys?"

"Yessir." I had never heard a black man say "yessir" to a black man.

"Yeah?" He turned to a woman in the car. "Hey, Woman, look who is here?"

I couldn't see her face. "Cuffy's children."

Then he leaned down to me.

"You got a great daddy, and don't you mind what anybody tell you about him. He is a great guy! You understand?"

"Yessir."

Felton grabbed my arm.

"Come on, let's go!"

I had to be dragged away. Looking back, I saw him leaning against the car, looking at us and laughing again with his head turned to the sky.

"Who is that?" I asked Felton as soon as we were out of hearing distance.

"That's Ezell Bannister! He's a gangster!" he said with admiration. "He is wanted in seven states. The white policeman tried to catch him, but they can't."

"What did he do?"

"I don't know . . . He did everything you could think of. He's a gangster! Once the police tried to stop him with a roadblock, but he was too smart for them. He cut through the woods and took another road. It was in the newspaper."

"What else did he do?"

"They say one time the law was after him, and he ran into Bob Kersey's house and put on one of Rockie's dresses, Rockie is Bob Kersey's wife, and come out and sat on the front porch, and crossed his legs. The policeman came up to him and asked him if he had seen a man driving a yellow car, and Ezell said no and the law went on."

"Where was the car?"

"Oh, he had parked it behind the house."

"But he knows my real daddy."

"Yeah, but your real daddy was a gangster too."

"He was! He was a gangster!"

"Yeah, but you better not tell your Uncle Lofton I told you."

When we got back to the warehouse, Uncle Lofton was talking to Rex Squire, the most famous horse dealer in five counties. Rex Squire had a deformed face; two black holes marked the place where he should have had a nose. My brother and I stared at his face with a feeling of horror mixed with awe. When we were around white people, my brother and I noticed any slight difference between them and ourselves. We specialized in physical deformities. If we saw a white person with a missing arm or leg, we'd call Aunt Amanda's attention to it. If we saw a humpbacked white person, we talked about it endlessly. Now standing before a white man with no nose, we could hardly contain our excitement.

After we walked off, Aunt Amanda leaned down and said, in an angry voice, "Doncha know to act! Don't be pickin at folks. White people can't help how God made em!"

We followed Uncle Lofton over to where the auctioneer was bidding for tobacco. I was fascinated by the rapid way he talked. Picking up a bundle of tobacco, he turned it over, sniffed it, threw it back, and called out a string of numbers. "Ninetyfive-ninetyfive-ninety-seventy-seventy-ninety-seventy! twice, sold, sold, SOLD to Philip Morris!—"

When he came to Uncle Lofton's tobacco, he bidded it for "Ninety-three!"

"Ninety-three!" Uncle Lofton exclaimed. "No, sir! I'll turn the tag on that!" He picked the tag up and turned it over. "Come, boys," he said. "Help me load it up!"

He scooted the tobacco onto a cart and took it across the warehouse to where Chesterfield bought their tobacco. The same auctioneer was coming down the row where Uncle Lofton had just put his tobacco. Uncle Lofton waited for him again.

This time he picked up the same tobacco and said, "Ninety-nine! One *hundred*! . . . Sold! To Chesterfield!"

"That's all right!" Uncle Lofton said, satisfied. "That's a lot better!"

When I asked him why the auctioneer didn't give him the price he wanted when he first looked at it, Uncle Lofton said that they didn't always realize how high the quality was the first time. He always showed them the same tobacco at least twice.

After he had sold his tobacco, we went to downtown Whiteville to buy my school clothes.

But I was unhappy because I wanted a convertible car even more now because Ezell Bannister had one. I thought that if I had enough money I could buy a car like this, and I would keep it until I was big enough to drive it.

"Why do you still want a car?"

"Because Ezell Bannister got one," I told him, completely forgetting that I had promised Felton that I wouldn't tell Uncle Lofton we had met him.

"How do you know what Ezell Bannister got?"

"Cause we saw him in his car!"

"Who showed you Ezell Bannister?"

"We saw him, when we went to get the orange drinks!"

"Now, son, you don't want nothin that Ezell Bannister got. He ain't nobody for you to imitate."

"But I want a car like his," I insisted.

"You need a lot of money to buy a car like that," Aunt Amanda said. "How you reckon you gonna get that much money?"

"I'll work for it!"

Aunt Amanda laughed. "Alright, you want to work and get some money?"

"Yeah."

"Do you want to come and work with me again and get you some money?" she asked. "You want to come pick star grass with me?"

I said I did, but I didn't know what she was talking about. Weren't we going to pick any more of Mr. Sam Dallason's cotton?

"We done picked all that man's cotton. The cotton season is gone. You gonna start school soon."

The next morning, as we drove to pick star grass, I questioned Aunt Amanda on how much money I would make. I asked her what star grass was, and she tried to explain it to me, but I really didn't understand what it was. When we arrived I saw several men burning the woods. As we got out of the car and moved closer, I saw that other black people, mostly women, were looking down in the areas where the woods had been freshly burned.

"Look! There's some star grass!" Aunt Amanda said. I saw something shiny in the dark, burnt debris. Aunt Amanda plucked up the shiny plant. It had leaves that shot off like porcupine quills. As I looked closer, I saw Aunt Amanda's hands rip off the long, thin green leaves until she held a small root between her fingers. I took the hard white root in my fingers to examine it.

"That's star grass," she said. "Us pick that and sell it to that white man up in Bolton and make us some money!"

"Yeah, this star grass pays right good," somebody else said.

"What's it for?" I asked.

"They make medicine out of that. You know that awful medicine you have to take when you have a cold?"

"Uh-huh."

"Well, that's one of the medicines they use it for," she said, unfolding a croker sack. "But it's good medicine if you just take it right from the ground like this. And mix in a little pine needle. Then, mix in a lot of merlin. That's what I give you and Knee when you are sick with a cold."

"These white folks use this stuff for penicillin," another woman said.

When the 2:55 blew, we took the star grass to the depot. A white man came out and put it all in a scale. When he finished, he counted out Aunt Amanda's money to her. She got a dollar a pound for the star grass. She gave me and my brother a dollar apiece for all the star grass we had picked.

That Saturday, Aunt Amanda took us to a toy shop in

Whiteville and showed me all the toy cars. "Now which automobile do you want?" she asked, pointing to all of the toys. I saw a small yellow convertible car just like the one Ezell Bannister had.

"That one!"

"Well, you now have enough money to buy it."

We took the car to the counter. My brother picked out a tractor. We paid for the toys with the money we had earned picking cotton and digging star grass. Later I played a fantasy game involving my father and Ezell in the role of gangsters, escaping from the police in their shiny convertible car.

Chapter 7

On Monday, September 9, 1949, Aunt Amanda drove me and Kenny Melvin to the schoolhouse. From the car window, the white school, not much bigger than a normal four-room house, materialized before me. Children in bright-colored clothes milled on the green lawn and around the white steps.

Aunt Amanda stopped the car, ordered me and Kenny out, and nudged us toward the school yard. "Now go on to school," she said. "Yonder is Miss Williams now, waiting for you. *Youuhooo!*"

A short, pretty woman waved back.

"Here comes Morris and Kenny!" Aunt Amanda yelled to her.

"Come on, Morris and Kenny," the woman said.

I crossed the green lawn and went to Miss Williams. I looked up into her face. I felt delight. She wore a blue dress trimmed with white lace. "Hello, Morris," she said to me. "Are you ready for school?"

I guessed I was. I had my Hopalong Cassidy lunch box. I had on my new clothes.

"Well, let's go to the classroom," she said, and took my hand. With eagerness, I took her hand, turning to see Knee waving from the car. Why did I feel so sad? Did I have to stay in school all day? I was going to ask Miss Williams these questions, but just at that moment, we entered the classroom. Why was it so large? Where were all the other children coming from?

"Now you sit here, Morris." I found my chair and placed my lunch box under the seat as I saw other children doing. I looked around at the other kids, especially the pretty girls. I found Kenny and tried to get his attention, but he didn't see me until I shouted his name out.

"No, no, we don't shout in school," Miss Williams said. I felt bad. I decided not to say anything for a while.

"Now, class, our first lesson!" Miss Williams said. "We will learn to read!"

She took out a big black book. When she untied the strings and opened the book, I saw a picture of Dick and Jane in a car with their parents, a white mother and father, and Spot the dog running after the car. Beneath the caption, written in very large bold letters, was "Dick saw Spot. See Spot run!"

As soon as I saw the words, I threw up my hands.

"What is it, Morris?"

"I can read it!"

"Oh, you can?" she asked incredulously.

"Yes, I can!"

She had a long thin stick with a rubber tip on it which she pointed under the word *Dick*.

"What does that say?"

"Dick saw Spot," I said, blurting out the whole sentence.

"Who else? Nobody else?" she asked, looking over the heads of the students. When she didn't see any more raised hands, she turned to me.

She called me to her desk.

"You put the pointer under the words, like I did, so that the rest of the class can read the words. Okay?"

I placed the pointer under the words while the students read them out loud. Miss Williams sat at her desk writing on a piece of paper. She occasionally would look up and smile at me.

I was so pleased with myself that when recess came I didn't want to go out of the room. I didn't want to leave her.

"Who parted your hair like that? Your mother?"

"No, I did. I don't have no mother."

"Oh, yes you do. What about Amanda?"

"She ain't my mamma."

"But she is like a mother to you, isn't she?"

"I don't know."

She turned and shook the grate in the wooden stove and the fire flared. "Where is your father?"

"In Virginia."

"What is he doing there?"

"I don't know. I got two fathers."

"You do?"

"Yeah—Uncle Lofton is my daddy and Culphert is my real father. Number one is Daddy and number two is father."

She laughed. "Now who told you this?"

"Nobody, I thought about it myself."

"Now go out and play with the other children," she ordered. I went outside but still watched her. She and Mr. Powell began to play croquet on the lawn. I felt jealous that he played with Miss Williams.

Then I ran to Willie Melvin over by the coal bin, a wooden shack with a truckload size of coal, on the other side of the school, where no girls were ever allowed to come, and where the big boys with weapons like pop-shooters, corn-shooters, slingshots, even BB guns, hung out.

"We making a slingshot," Willie told me. "Earl Beatty is gonna show us."

I watched the boy cut a tongue from an old shoe and fasten a rubber sling cut from an inner tube to each end. He put a rock in it and slung it up beside the coal house. It made a dent as deep as a BB gun would make.

Behind the schoolhouse and not far from the coal bin was the Jukes house. I saw Juicy Belle sitting on the porch with a white man. Already I had heard that people did bad things in that house, but I didn't understand what that meant.

Mr. Powell stood on the steps and rang the school bell and I saw the children running inside.

That afternoon, in the classroom again, after we had laid our heads on the desk for a nap, we played the button game. We were supposed to hold our hands together on our desk. One pupil put the button in his hand and went around to all of the students slipping his hand between the other hands.

When he was finished, we had to guess who had the button. When Vandyke, another boy who couldn't read at all, came around to my desk, I thought he would give it to me. Hadn't I helped him with the word *mutt*? But he didn't. I was so disappointed that I cried.

"Now stop that, Morris?" Miss Williams said.

"He didn't give it to me," I cried.

51

"But maybe the next time somebody will give it to you. I tell you what, why don't you pass the button out?"

This felt better. I liked running up and down the aisle with the button in my hand. This was more fun than I had ever had. I liked the power to decide who got the button.

I put the button in Kenny's hand, but he giggled so loud everybody knew it. With such obvious complicity, the game soon ended. It was just as well because the school bell rang and my first day of school came to an end.

Aunt Amanda was there waiting when we came down the steps. In the car she asked me how I liked school and I was quick to reply that I liked it, remembering the excitement of so many faces, names, and games I had played. But I was really impressed by our teacher; she was so pretty and nice.

"How did you like school today?" Uncle Lofton asked me later.

"I liked it," I told him.

"Oh, he was jumping for joy," Aunt Amanda said. "Just jumping for joy!"

"We picked us a lot of star grass today," Knee told me.

"I goin to get me a slingshot," I told him. He wanted to know if he could get one. I told him about the adventure near the coal bin, explaining all the dangerous and forbidden things the big boys did.

I was so excited about going to school that the next day I asked to be taken early. I was so early that only a few pupils were already there.

After I had helped Miss Williams with the big black book, she asked me, "Do you like helping me?"

"Yes, ma'am."

"Okay, now come here."

She pulled out her shoeshine box and sat down in the chair near the fire and put her foot up on the box.

"Do you know how to do it? Here, I'll show you."

I kneeled down in front of her shoeshine box and she opened the can of brown polish for me.

"Now you put a little polish on the cloth, and then put it on the shoe and put it all over."

"Okay."

"Be careful that you don't put any of it on my leg. Don't spill it."

"Okay."

"And when you finish with that, take this brush and brush them like this." She demonstrated the brushing.

"Okay."

She leaned back with the *Star News* and I started polishing her shoe. She had her legs up and I looked under her dress. With the fire roaring and the morning light so clear and the room so empty and the silence between us, it was pure joy.

I must have been looking so long and hard that I forgot to apply the motion of my cloth on her brown patent-leather shoes, for she moved the newspaper from her face and looked down at me with curiosity.

"What are you looking at so hard?" she asked gently.

"Nothing," I said and resumed my motions on her shoe.

"Now, that's enough polish. Take the brush and brush them."

She went back to her newspaper and didn't say anything for a while. A long silence passed between us and I thought she was asleep.

The door opened suddenly and Miss Williams jumped up. Vandyke ran into the room.

"Good morning, Miss Williams!"

"Vandyke, you are so rude! Sit down!" she screamed at him. "Be a nice boy, like Morris." Then she said to me, "Morris, thank you for the shoeshine. Here." She took out a nickel and gave it to me. I put it in my pocket. She touched me on the head and said, "Now put the book out for the class and lead the devotion."

I opened the Dick and Jane book in front of the class as the pupils rushed into the room and took their seats.

"Everybody rise," I said, "and sing the Negro National Anthem."

The class started singing the song. After we finished with the first song, I said, "Now, let's say a prayer."

"But you have to ask somebody," Miss Williams said.

"James Randell please say a prayer."

James Randell, a tall, very black pupil who was usually quiet, stood up, and to my surprise, he gave a good prayer to God.

"Now, that's the end of devotion."

"So when you and Cathleen gonna get married," Uncle Lofton said to Elmo, as we sat down to dinner that late afternoon.

53

He grinned shyly.

"I ain't asked her yet," he said.

"She sure is a pretty gal," Aunt Amanda said. She was wearing her starched white uniform. She was going to work at the Anchorage Club.

"She sho is," Uncle Lofton said. "If you love her you ought to marry her."

Aunt Amanda looked at Elmo's plate. He hadn't touched his food.

"He must be in love, cause look at his plate. Ain't touched a thing!" She laughed out loud and Elmo just looked sheepishly down at the chicken on his plate.

"Can I have your chicken?" I asked him. What was it, this love, that could cause Elmo not to want to eat his fried chicken? But it must be something like the measles because he looked ashy around the face. Until now Elmo had been a normal person, always having fun with me and Knee. Suddenly, he had come down with love and couldn't even eat his chicken.

"Yeah," he said and I grabbed it.

"Give you brother some," Uncle Lofton told me, and I pulled off a piece of the wing and threw it on Knee's plate.

"Now, that ain't the way to hand something to your own brother," Uncle Lofton said. "Treat yo brother like yo brother." I had to take the piece of wing up and gently hand it to my brother.

"Now that's better."

"Daddy, can I go with Elmo?" I asked. I became so preoccupied with love that I wanted to see Elmo's girlfriend Cathleen. Was she pretty as Miss Williams? As Ruth Spann? As two other girls in my class, like Barbara Ann? and Violet Mae?

"Where's Elmo going?"

I looked over at him.

"Elmo, ain't you going to see Cathleen?"

"Uh-huh."

"See there, Uncle Lofton, he is going to see Cathleen. Can I go?"

"And me too?"

"No, Knee, you can go the next time. Morris, you can go with Elmo."

Knee started crying.

"All right, you both can go. But first you take in the clothes and then do your homework and then you can go."

We rushed from the table to the kitchen, plucked up the basket, and went to the backyard. Knee took the pole that propped up the line so that I could reach them. I took the clothespins off the clothes and let them fall to the ground.

"Don't let them clothes fall on the ground, boy!" Elmo shouted to me. He was in the backyard with his goat.

As we put the clothes into the basket, I told Knee about the spit-shooter the other boys had in school. A spit gun was a home-made toy that was the rage among the boys at school. A hollow cane was stuffed on one end with a wad of spit-soaked paper, and a ramp was inserted in the other end with another. When you pushed the ramp into the hollow cane, the pressure caused the spitball to shoot out of the other end. We would take the spitball and aim it at somebody's head.

"You gonna get me one too?"

"Yeah, we can kill birds with it," I lied, looking at Aunt Amanda's panties on the line. I decided to pass over them and left them hanging.

We brought the fluffy clean clothes into the house. Aunt Amanda had the ironing board out and was ironing.

"Put them right here so I can get them," she said. "Did you get everything?"

"Yes, Mamma."

She turned her head and looked out the back door and saw that the only thing hanging on the line was her underwear.

"Why did you leave my things on the line for?"

"I don't want to touch them," I said.

"You don't want to what?"

"They nasty!"

"Nasty?" she laughed. "Lofton, come here!"

Uncle Lofton came and she pointed to her underwear hanging on the line and they both laughed. I felt ashamed and embarrassed.

"Hahahaha! Them boys say those things nasty." Uncle Lofton laughed again just as Elmo came up.

"Y'all ready to go?" he said to me and Knee. "Cause I'm ready."

He turned to Uncle Lofton and Aunt Amanda. "I'm gonna take the car and pick up Cathleen and get her some ice cream."

"Okay, be careful with my car," Aunt Amanda said to him.

"I will, don't worry."

We ran out and jumped into the car.

Before Elmo picked up Cathleen, he stopped by J. C. Himes Place, a juke joint where young black men hung out.

Junior Jenkins was shooting pool. Bug-eyed Bill Collins and my Uncle Lindsey also held pool sticks.

"Hey!" speaking to Elmo.

"Hey, you self!"

"Don't say nothin to Junior Jenkins, man, he tryin to concentrate. If you talk too loud, he can't shoot the cue ball!" Bug-eyed Bill Collins said, dragging on a cigarette. He had eyes that dripped down like a waxed candle. Everybody called him Bug-eyed because of the way his eyes ran down his face.

"Lissen here, Bug-eyed Bill Collins," Junior Jenkins said, rising from his stance at the pool table. "I can concentrate, boy! I got a big brain!"

"Then go head and shoot, fool," Lindsey said.

"Now look a heah, Lindsey, a cotton stalk too close to the weed will find the hoe gives it no head!" Junior Jenkins reminded him.

"Shoot an stop yapping, fool," another man said.

"I'm Joe Louis," Junior Jenkins said, and took the shot. He missed. "I'm Joe Louis!" he said again, and turned to us. "That's right, Joe Fucking Louis!"

"You ain't dooleesque!" Bug-eyed Bill said, taking up his pool stick.

Junior Jenkins spread his legs, jacked his pants up to his crotch, and recited an ode to Joe Louis:

"One dark Saturday night twentyfifth of March
Joe Louis kissed his wife at the studio gate
He said, 'Baby, I hate to leave you 'cause m running late!'
Joe Louis jumped in the ring with his gloves on
Said he beat every motherfucker on the promise land
Max Schmeling rose at the sound of the bell,
Joe Louis knocked his just as flat as hell
He said, 'Son, to beat me you got to get up and go!
My ass is big and black and my teeth shine like pearl
I'm a ugly m.f., but *I'm the champion of the world.*' "

"You ain't no Joe Louis!" Uncle Lindsey said. "Don't care what you say! I ought to know, cause a bullfrog knows more about the weather than an almanac. I'm that bullfrog."

"Hell, if you Joe Louis, I'm Stagolee," Lindsey vowed. "Y'all know what Staggerlee did, don't you? He killed Billy Lyon."

"Sho nuf!" Bug-eyed Bill Collins said. "Kilt him with a smoke-less forty-fo!"

Lindsey rested the pool stick on his toe and said, "I'll tell you about Stagolee:

It was a cold and dark night
When Stagolee and Billy Lyon had that awful fight
They were two men gambling, Billy threw seven
Stagolee swore he threw eight
Billy had won Stagolee's Stetson hat
Stagolee said, 'Billy, I can't let you go with that!'
He pulled out his smokeless .44
Said, 'You ain't going to cheat me no mo'.'
Billy said, 'Please, Stag, don't take my life
I got two children and po sickly wife.'
Stagolee said, 'I don't care about your children and wife
I saw you hold out that ace on me, I'm gonna take your life!'
Stagolee shot Billy, he shot that boy so bad
That the bullet went throw him and broke the bartender's glass
Then Stagolee walked out the bar
But he didn't get far,
A policeman named Frisbie arrested and took him to jail.
And nobody was there to go his bail
When Stagolee's wife heard the news
She was sitting on her bed lacing up her shoes
She went to the judge with a handful of nickels and dimes
But the judge said, 'I'm gonna make an example of Stagolee
I'm gonna give him a lot of time to think about his crime!'
When the day of Stagolee's trial came around
None of his friends could be found
The judge said, 'Stagolee, I can tell you are a bad man
By the redness in your eye!
I'm gonna sentence you to ten years in jail!'
Stagolee put out his chest and said, 'Ninety-nine ain't no time!
My grand daddy is in Sing Sang doing Ninety-nine!' "

"That bad Stagolee!" Elmo yelled. The other men howled their approval of Stagolee's exploits. I was convinced that this Stagolee was my father, and the narrative was a description of what my father had done.

"Who's boy is that?" a black man who walked in the door said.

"That's Cuffy's boy," Lindsey told him.

"Cuffy? Cuffy Brown?" He looked down at me and my brother,

taking a closer interest in us. "Now, boy, talking about a bad nigger. That Cuffy is a real Stagolee!"

"Ha, ha, ha! Yeah, he sho is!"

The man looked at me again and laughed. "Boy, you daddy is a bad nigger. Is you gonna be a bad nigger like your daddy?"

Lindsey stepped in. "Don't tell him that!" He turned to Junior Jenkins and told him to go ahead and make his shot.

Suddenly I felt I knew more about my father than I had ever known. Their gestures, their language, their looks, and their glances told me that my father was a hero to them. I now was one of them. I felt a deep respect for my father. As the men continued their game, I couldn't help but be moved by the revelations of my father's reputation. This was the first time I had heard that my father had killed somebody—or had he?

Junior Jenkins shot the eight ball in the pocket and picked up the money from the pool table.

"Junior got more money than A. J. Harris!" Bug-eyed Bill said. "All from cheating us with this pool game."

"Hell, a fool can make money, but it takes a wise man to spend it," Elmo said. "All Junior gonna do is give it back to Heads and Tails for wine."

"You don't think old Jack Harris know how to spend all that money he makes off that railroad? Shucks, sho do! See that big brick house he built!"

"Hell, he could do better than goin around to the Jukes place and spending it on poontang!" Lindsey chortled with laughter.

"They said Mrs. Harris don't even have a poontang," Junior said.

"They said a man come there in Jack Harris shoe, and said, 'I'd like a jar of syrup.' Mrs. Harris say, 'Why, we don't have that.' The man say, pointing to a jar of it sitting on the counter, 'Yes, you do! It's sitting right there!' Mrs. Harris say, 'Why, that's what we call *molasses*.' Say, 'Folks change the names of things so much, you never know what they talking about half the time.' Say, 'A fellow came in hair they other day, and ask me for some *poontang*, and I declare, I didn't know what he was talkin about. *I probably have a lot of poontang and don't even know it!*'"

The men chuckled and said "poontang" to each other several times as if it were a magic word.

"Elmo, what's poontang?" I asked him.

"Poontang," he laughed. "Morris wants to know what a poontang is? He likes to polish Miss Williams's shoes. Hahahaha!" I had told him this before, but now I was ashamed.

"Who? Miss Williams?"

"Boy, she's finer than frog's hair!"

". . . Say, there was this woman who use to be married to Dick Yeoman. You remember how fine she was!"

"Oh, man, she was fine, and he didn't even know what to do with her, except give her money."

"Yeah, well she went shopping over here in Why-ville. She wanted to get a shoeshine. She got up on this shoe stand, you know. And that stand was high, you know. So, the shoeshine man was shining her shoes and looked up between her legs and saw that poontang and said, *Lady, I could eat it full of ice cream!*' So the lady come on back to Bolton to her husband, and told her husband what this shoeshine man had said. Her husband was mad. She said, 'Why you mad? You should go back over there and hit him upside his head. If you loved me you'd do it.' So Dick Yeoman said, you know how he talked, in that high voice, 'You had no business in Why-ville in the first place. And in the second place, you had no business up on that shoeshine stand. And in the third place, *can't nobody eat that much ice cream!*"

Elmo and the rest of the boys broke out laughing, but I didn't understand. I thought they were still talking about Miss Williams asking me to shine her shoes. I was angry that they even talked about Miss Williams like that, saying she was "fine" and she had ice cream between her legs.

"Well, see you guys later," Elmo said, and we followed him out of the hall. In the car on the way to Cathleen, I questioned him further about poontang.

"Poontang, man, is what girls have and it's good too!"

"Can you eat it?"

"Naw, man, you don't eat it, you git some!"

"How you get it?"

"Put yo dick in it, that's how! It feels good too!"

"It's nasty, ain't it?"

"No, it ain't nasty, unless the girl don't wash it. If she don't wash it, it stinks. But it's still good. See, you take you dick out and stick it in."

"But Ruth Spann won't let me stick it in her."

"You have to find one who will."

"Will Cathleen let you stick your thing in her?"

He hauled off and slapped me.

"What you hit me for."

"Don't you talk dirty about my girl, boy, I'm gonna marry her."

"Is it bad if a girl lets you stick your thing in her?"

"It ain't bad if she loves you."

"Cathleen loves you?"

"I hope so," he said, not sounding too sure.

When we got to Cathleen's house, Elmo went inside and me and Knee stayed in the car. Soon he came back with Cathleen. As I looked at this beautiful light-skinned girl of about eighteen, dressed in red pedal pushers, her hair scooped up so nice and tied with a yellow ribbon, I wished she loved me too. I would get me a girlfriend like Cathleen.

"Get out of the car and get in the backseat," he commanded us, and we jumped in the back.

"Hello, Morris and Knee," Cathleen said.

"Hi."

As we drove along in the car, I said, "Cathleen, Elmo said he wanted to stick his thing in you and get some poontang." Was I taking revenge on him and the other boys for what they said about Miss Williams? I didn't know, I just opened my mouth and the words came out. But as soon as they were out of my mouth, I saw Cathleen's face redden, and her hand covered her mouth quickly. Then Elmo's head dropped suddenly, and he glanced over at Cathleen. His mouth moved like a little fish gasping for air, but no words came out.

"Morris got a real filthy mouth," he said finally, and then laughed. "Don't be surprised if you hear some bad words coming out of his mouth."

Cathleen didn't say anything anymore, just turned red and looked hard at Elmo. Knee and I laughed because Elmo wanted to hit me, but he wouldn't do it with Cathleen there. I realized that he would take his revenge by not buying us any ice cream.

"Morris," she said after a while, "so you know a lot of bad words?"

"Yes, ma'am!"

"Who taught you those words?"

"Uncle Elmo!" My brother and I laughed.

We stopped at the Dairy Queen for some ice cream. Elmo did buy us ice cream, but with just one glance at him, I could tell he was still mad.

In school the next day we were playing pass the button again. The girl who had the button was Ruth Spann, the most beautiful girl in the world. She had dark brown skin and was cute. Suddenly I realized that it was she who was to be my girlfriend, like Cathleen was Elmo's girlfriend.

When she came to my desk, I put my hands together, palm to palm, as we were supposed to do. She slipped her folded hands which contained the button into mine and I waited for it to fall into my hand. When you loved somebody you gave them the button. But she didn't give it to me. Didn't she love me?

"Gimme me the button!" I whispered, thinking that she had forgotten to let it go. "What's wrong with you?" Why didn't she act like Cathleen did to Elmo, like she was supposed to, smile at me, be nice to me, and give me that button?

"No!" she yelled.

She tried to pull her hand from mine.

"Give it to me!"

"No!"

"Listen," I whispered, "if you don't give me the button, then give me some *poontang*."

Her hand flew to her mouth.

"I'm gonna tell!" she promised. I watched her, horrified, as she marched up to Miss Williams. She whispered into her ear.

Miss Williams immediately stopped the game and imposed an emergency. She strutted in front of the class and announced that a "boy had said something bad."

"Come here," she said, opening my hand by pinching my fingers back. As I watched, she took out the ruler. The first whack of that ruler began a long series of punishments I was to receive as part of my southern education.

"Now tell me what poontang is?" she asked. She was not so much younger than Aunt Amanda. But her authority over me was different. I was ashamed before a woman for the first time.

"Tell me what *poontang* is?"

I dropped my head. I didn't know what poontang was. *Bad boy, just like your daddy.*

"Have you ever *seen* a poontang?"

"No, ma'am."

"Then why did you *ask* Ruth for some?"

"I don't know."

"You don't know?"

"No, ma'am."

"Don't you know that it's a *bad* word?"

"Yes, ma'am!"

She had been holding my fingers and now she gave me ten licks on the open palm with the ruler.

I cried, and everybody, everybody who mattered, Ruth, Barbara Anne, Violet May, laughed at me.

She grabbed me by the nape of the neck and shoved me under her desk and held me between her legs and went on with the class. As she went on with the instruction to the rest of the class, she loosened her leg grip on my head and I sat down and stared under her dress.

I studied the black nylon stockings and the garter clasp. Up further, I could see where the stockings ended and where her dark flesh began. I could smell her sexual odor.

"Come on out," I heard Miss Williams say. She stood up and I came out. There was another teacher with her, Mrs. Garden.

"He is so bad," Miss Williams said. "Let me tell you what he did!"

Mrs. Garden was a big fat teacher. Her bosom started at her neck and ballooned out and curved down at her waist. She stood there patiently listening to the charges against me, punctuating her dissatisfaction with an occasional glance down at me.

"Now do you know what poontang is?" she laughed.

I shook my head. If it was so bad, why did they laugh about it?

"Now you can go home," Miss Williams said, "and tell Amanda to send me a mess of them mustard."

"Okay."

When I came in from school, Aunt Amanda asked me, standing near the refrigerator drinking her clabber milk, how school was. I followed her into the living room, where some singing was coming from the radio.

"I don't like Miss Williams," I cried. "She hit me!"

"What did you do? You must have done something bad."

"No, I didn't."

"Come in this kitchen. I got something for you to eat."

"We went to the kitchen table where Uncle Lofton and Elmo were already seated and took our places.

"I'm gonna ask Miss Williams what you did bad," Aunt Amanda said as she served the chicken. "She will tell me."

I felt sorry that I had even brought the whole thing up now. The next time, I told myself, I won't say anything to Aunt Amanda. I wasn't even going to tell her that Miss Williams said to send her some mustard greens.

"She said send her some muster greens," I said, forgetting my anger.

The next morning, I woke up early and saw pellets of rain hitting on the windowpane. Outside it was still dark. This was one of those dark, cold November days in North Carolina that sometimes turned into hurricanes. But did it matter what the weather was like when I had to polish Miss Williams's shoes?

The floor was like ice as I got out of bed. It was cold in the house too. When I came into the living room I saw that Uncle Lofton had started a fire in the wood stove.

"Daddy, I got to get to school!"

"Boy, can't you see it's raining outside. We can't hardly let you go out there in this weather."

"But I got to go, Daddy!"

"We can't get the car in this weather. It'll get stuck in the mud."

"I got to go there!" I started crying.

By that time, Elmo had gotten up. "I'll take him on the mare," he said.

From another part of the house, still in bed, Aunt Amanda said, "You gonna take him to school on the back of the old horse, eh? Well, that's the way we use to go everywhere."

The idea of riding on the back of the horse to school didn't particularly appeal to me, but it didn't matter as long as I got there before the other students and had Miss Williams alone.

"Hurry up, then!" I demanded.

I could hear Elmo's high cackle of a laugh. "Boy, you sho bossy this morning."

I rushed into the bathroom and pulled off my stocking cap—I had taken to sleeping in a stocking cap which was a piece of Aunt

Amanda's nylon stocking, so that my hair would be wavy and slick. I ran water in the sink and started applying thick globs of Royal Crown grease to my hair like I'd seen Elmo do when he went to see Cathleen. I parted my hair on the side, like he had his.

"Aunt Amanda, where is my pants?" I yelled.

"Just a minute, little man," she said, and picked up my pants from the ironing board and handed them to me.

"I can't wear them." I pouted.

"What's wrong now?"

"You didn't crease them."

"Boy, you so particular! Give 'em to me!"

She put them on the ironing board again and heated the iron, and while it was heating, she went into the kitchen and turned the grits off.

By the time I had eaten the grits, sausages, and eggs and drunk the big glass of milk, I had another anxiety attack: I realized that if I rode the horse to school, I would spoil the creases in my pants. I wanted Miss Williams to see the sharp, long, clean line in my pants.

"Aunt Amanda," I said, looking out the window and seeing Elmo on the horse in the front yard, "I can't go on the horse."

"Why can't you go on the horse?"

"My pants will get messed up."

"Well, then, you stay yo butt home."

"But I got to go!"

"Then make up your mind—what you want to do? Go or stay? You can see that we can't drive the car through them muddy roads. Now, listen. When I was a little girl, we didn't have the chance to go to school. We had to work, even when we were little like you. Now, we doin all we can to see that you get an education."

Uncle Lofton came to me.

"Here, put this over you," he said, and I turned and saw that he had a large piece of canvas that they used to cover the tobacco when they took it to the market.

"Ain't nobody in your family ever cared that much about education," he said. "Look at me. I ain't been to school but a few days in my life!" He had cut a hole in it for my head and the rest of it was wide enough to cover all of me.

"This boy is like Booker T. Washington. He wants to go to school so bad that he will ride a horse to school!" he went on.

64

"Okay," I said, satisfied, as I held up my head. Then he put a rain hat with a large brim on my head so that my greased conk would be protected too.

They led me to the front porch, and Uncle Lofton heisted me up on the horse's back. "We are so proud of you!" Aunt Amanda said, putting a brown paper bag of vegetables in my arm for Miss Williams. She went back to the porch. "Nobody can say that you didn't have a chance for your education."

"Bye, bye, Morris," Uncle Lofton yelled as Lizzie moved off down the road.

"Bye!"

I watched Lizzie's big gray feet plop into the mud. She was a gray mare all right, but in the morning drizzle she looked as white as a ghost. Her back was as broad as a bed and her movements as rhythmic as a seesaw. The air was clean and smelled full of the pine trees that blew in the early-morning wind. The rain poured down on me, but I felt insulated, warm, and happy.

Chapter 8

One cold day in November, a few weeks before Thanksgiving, I found myself in the backseat of the car being hurried along to our father in prison. As we sat in the visiting room with my father, I again felt aware of the sadness that invaded the room. I was now old enough to realize how unpleasant the situation was. He asked me if I had been good, as I promised I would be. Before I answered him, I remembered the turkey incident, the poontang incident with Miss Williams, the fight with my cousin Eli. I had tried to be good, I wanted to tell him, but I only managed to say, "Yes. I've been good." Yet I knew that he had been a bad nigger, as Ezell Bannister and the man in the poolroom had referred to him. When we left him that day, I was confused. I wanted to keep my father's promise to be good, but I also wanted to be like him, a bad nigger.

It was difficult to reconcile this "bad" reputation with the kind nature which he projected in his letters home to us and in his gentleness when we visited him in prison.

When we got back to Bolton, Mr. Roy Melvin came to Uncle Lofton and told him that he had somebody he wanted to meet.

"These fellows is some *good* gospel singers," Mr. Roy Melvin told Aunt Amanda as they stood in the kitchen with me and Knee.

I didn't know what a gospel singer was, but I was eager to find out.

"They call themselves the Gospel Two," he said.

We got in the car and headed off to meet them.

"My eye been itching all morning," Aunt Amanda said, glancing out the car window, "and I knew that we was going to get some company."

Uncle Lofton stopped the car in front of the church. Two men stood by the sycamore tree.

"Is that them?" Daddy asked.

"Yes sir, Buddy," Mr. Roy Melvin said. "That's the Gospel Two!"

We got out of the car to meet them.

"Smilin' Henry," Mr. Roy Melvin said, turning from the man to Uncle Lofton. "Lofton Freeman."

"Howdy," Daddy said.

I was already out of the car, closing in on Smilin' Henry. He was a tall, light-skinned man in his thirties, about Uncle Lofton's age, with slick hair, sideburns, and a mustache.

When he came around the car to shake hands with Uncle Lofton, I looked at his shoes. I always judged people's character by the shoes they wore. Where had I seen brown and white two-tone shoes before? Brown on the toes and white on the sides? The Sears Roebuck catalogue! I had seen shoes like this on white people! Could Negroes wear white shoes? Could they get them on their feet?

"And this is Carl Mack."

Carl Mack was darker but he had the same thick mustache, slick hair, and sideburns.

"These are some fellows," Roy Melvin said to Daddy. "Some gospel singers looking for a church to sing in."

"Pleased to meet you," Daddy said.

I saw a picture of Smilin' Henry and Carl Mack nailed to the sycamore tree. The red letters printed on the white paper said, "Come hear the Gospel Two! The Greatest Gospel singers in the South Today! These boys really moan! Smilin' Henry's got the hip-slapping style! Carl Mack's got the flat-footed style. Together they praise the Lord in the best gospel you ever heard! Have them sing in your church today! Come! See! Hear! These Amazing Singers!!"

When I turned around, I saw Carl Mack talking to Aunt Amanda.

"We been singing all over."

"Oh, I love gospel music," Aunt Amanda said.

Smilin' Henry opened a bag and took out a rack, which he began to fasten to the top of our Hudson. Uncle Lofton took one end of the rack and helped him fasten it to the roof.

"What is it, Daddy?" I asked when I saw them hoist a cylinder onto the rack.

"That's a loudspeaker!"

"What's it for?"

"For singing! Singing the gospel!"

"That's right!"

"Uh-huh!"

After the loudspeaker was fixed securely on the car, we got in.

Daddy drove down the road to Outback, past our road and Mrs. Laura Melvin's house, which sat across the road from our mailbox. We stopped at Joe Howard's place. Smilin' Henry sat in the back of the car with the microphone, and as we drove up to the house, he started moaning.

Joe Howard, his wife, and his children came out on their porch and listened to the loudspeaker. Mr. Roy Melvin, Aunt Amanda, and Uncle Lofton joined in clapping their hands and singing along with them. Joe Howard and his wife started singing with them too. When they finished singing, Joe Howard came up to the car.

"What is this?"

"This is the Gospel Two. They are going to sing at our church. You better come down if you want to sing some more," Mr. Roy told him.

"I believe I will. When is that goin be?"

"Next Sunday," said Aunt Amanda. "And you better buy one of my pies. I'm trying to raise money to see if I can outrun the other women from the other churches trying to raise money."

Joe Howard said he would buy some of Aunt Amanda's pies. When we pulled off, they shouted and waved to us. Smilin' Henry sang as Daddy drove back on the road to John Smith's place. On both sides of the road, people were out in the cornfield cutting down the stalks, stacking them in piles, and setting them on fire. Around the blazes, people were dancing. It was not yet dark.

When they heard the singing, they turned from the fires and ran toward the car. They must have known the songs, because as the Gospel Two started singing, they sang back to our car.

Uncle Lofton stopped at John Smith's place. Mr. John Smith had a big, clean farm. The buildings were always painted white, and the lawns were cut. I felt the same quietness when I visited them as I did when I visited Sam Dallason's farm.

Mr. John Smith came out. He had blond hair and big blue eyes, but he was no white man.

We got out of the car, with Carl Mack and Smilin' Henry. "If you buy a pie from me, I guarantee you that I'll be the queen!" Aunt Amanda said.

"Mandy, you know I'm going to buy a pie from you," Mr. John Smith said, winking at me. "She makes the best pies in the world, don't she, Morris?"

The Gospel Two gave an impromptu concert right there. After they had sung five songs, Mr. Smith announced that Aunt Amanda was sure to win the contest because she had the fastest car, the Hudson.

I didn't understand what the contest was about, and that afternoon after we had finished singing, I asked Uncle Lofton. He told us that Aunt Amanda was trying to raise money for the gospel group, Carl Mack and Smilin' Henry. Her competition was women from other churches in Bolton. Each of them had a car. Mrs. Kersey, from the Green Chapel, had a Ford, Mrs. Cleo Smith from Shepard's Tabernacle had a Chevrolet, and Mrs. Mary Mostley from the Holiness had a Studebaker.

"But Manda got the Hudson," Daddy said, "and can't nobody beat that!"

Every afternoon after school that week I stood in the kitchen and watched Aunt Amanda make the pies she sold to raise money. I would sit there, waiting for the bowl to lick. It was pleasant and wonderful to watch her peel peaches, cut up the pieces, mix in pumpkin with lemon flour, nutmeg, butter, Carnation milk, and shove the pies in the oven. She would hand the bowl to us and we would sit on the floor and dip our fingers into the delicious pudding. Then we would take turns licking out the insides.

We rode around in the car a lot that week too. Aunt Amanda took the gospel singers wherever they needed to go to advertise their shows. Carl Mack and Smilin' Henry became my new role models. If I couldn't be like my father, then I could be like these singers who wore nice clothes and sang songs. I noticed how the people liked them, and if I was like them I wouldn't be like my bad father.

On Sunday, Aunt Amanda invited the Gospel Two to dinner.

She sent us to the garden to cut a mess of okra. We dashed into the kitchen and got the pan and knife from the kitchen, and with Knee following me, I ran into the vegetable garden behind the house. We passed the beanstalks, jumped over a big watermelon, and then came to the rows of okra. I hated cutting okra because

69

they had a prickly skin and it was impossible not to get the fine splinters in your hand when you cut them. But when Aunt Amanda cut them up in small pieces and put them in the butter beans, they were delicious to eat.

"Hold the pan up?" I demanded of my brothers as I reached up on the okra stalk and cut one of the green okra. I dropped the okra into the wobbly held pan.

I reached up on the stalk for another okra and felt my brother's hand dig into my skin. "Snake!" he screamed, dropping the pan and running. I looked down and saw the black, diamond-shaped head of the snake, his forked tongue spitting rapidly out of his mouth. I dashed to the house and picked up a hoe lying against the steps.

"Come on! Let's kill the snake," I yelled to Knee. He followed me back to where we had seen the snake. It was curled up near an okra stalk, and I hit at him with the hoe. Naturally he fought back, but I beat him with that hoe until I severed his head from his body. I felt I had accomplished a great victory and was very proud of what I had done.

We took the snake on the end of the hoe and carried him past the pond and into Mrs. Suzanne's yard. Willie and Kenneth came out to look at it. Willie took one look and said, "That's a king snake!"

"A king snake?"

He explained to me that a king snake was the worst snake to kill, because they had plenty of relatives, and that they were going to get me.

"Get me? For what?"

"For killing him. Do you think they gonna let you get away with this?" Willie asked calmly.

He explained that the king snake was the most vengeful snake there was. If it had been any other snake, I might have had a chance. If it had been a green snake, I wouldn't even have seen him; green snakes are not visible except in the middle of the day. If it had been a rattlesnake, the worst I could have expected would have been to have been hypnotized by his trembling tail. If it had been any other of the hundreds of snakes, I would have been okay because most snakes wouldn't even die until the sun went down, no matter how many times you might cut them up with a hoe.

"When will they come for me?" I asked.

"In the night . . . probably," he said.

"And put me in prison? Kill me?"

"Probably both."

"But my daddy Cuffy will come from prison and kill him," I informed Willie.

"He can't kill all of the snake's relatives."

"But my daddy Culphert will come out of the mountains and kill the snake!" I told him.

"Ain't Mr. Lofton Freeman your daddy?"

"Naw, I have another daddy," I informed him. "Didn't you hear about him? He is a mean man and can kill snakes."

"What y'all doing out there!" Aunt Amanda yelled from the back door of the kitchen. When I ran up to the house with the empty pan, she looked at me and shouted, "Where's the okra?"

"We killed a snake!"

She looked at me again and then looked down at my arms.

"What y'all doin in your Sunday clothes for anyway! Didn't I tell you to take off them Sunday clothes?"

"We killed a snake!" Knee exclaimed.

"I don't care what you killed! Get them Sunday clothes off! What you look like in your Sunday clothes killing anything!"

When we came out of our room where we had changed our clothes, I saw Daddy still talking to Smilin' Henry and Carl Mack.

"Is anybody hungry? I made somethin for us to eat," Aunt Amanda said.

"Yes," Smilin' Henry said, smiling broadly; he was always smiling except when he poked his feet under a dinner table where Aunt Amanda had spread out her buttermilk biscuits, butter beans and okra, candied sweet potatoes, collard greens, black-eyed peas, and smoked cured ham. Then he was all business, and a serious look, like a catfish emerging from muddied water, came over his light brown face.

As for Carl Mack, he was no slouch either. What a mouth he had on him. I watched globs of food disappear down his big cavern. You would never have imagined that they had ever eaten southern food in their lives.

While we men ate, Aunt Amanda sat at the table without eating a bit. It was always a mystery to me how she could live without eating, for I never saw her eat any food.

To finish off the meal, Aunt Amanda served us chocolate she had baked.

"I got to go to work," she said, rising and disappearing into the other room where she changed from her Sunday clothes into a starched white uniform. "Well, I'll be back around ten," she said.

Uncle Lofton told me and my brother to go to the watermelon patch and bring a watermelon.

"No, Daddy, I'm scared to go in the watermelon patch," I said.

"What you scared of?"

"Snakes?"

"You ain't never been scared of snakes before?"

Still we wouldn't budge. Daddy offered us orange soda pops from A. J. Harris's, but we declined. Finally he excused himself from the Gospel Two and went himself. We followed at a safe distance.

It was still light enough to see the path. We looked for snakes, any kind. They went out about this time of night, Willie told us, looking for water. Uncle Lofton picked out the biggest watermelon, placed his ear to it, gave it a thump to see if the inner heart had loosened up and was ready to be eaten. It was ready, he indicated with a nod. He plucked it from the vine and, hauling it up on his shoulder, headed back to the house; we ran back to the house in front of him.

Mr. Roy Melvin and Mr. Buster came up from the footpath.

After a long time of eating watermelon and spitting out seeds and slapping the mosquitoes, Buster said to Carl Mack, "How you gonna play music in the church? It ain't in the Bible."

"Yes, it is," Carl Mack said.

"We got a preacher in our church who says all this singing and mess ain't in the Bible. He says the Negroes shouldn't be singing and howlin and playin instruments in church."

"But he's crazy."

"Go get the Bible," Uncle Lofton told me. I dashed over to the old piano and took the Bible down.

I passed it to Uncle Lofton, who passed it to Carl Mack, who flipped through it like somebody who knew what he was doing, and then read out loud to us.

" 'Praise yea the Lord. Praise God in his sanctuary: praise him in the heaven of his power. Praise him for his mighty acts. Praise him according to his excellent greatness. Praise him wit the sound of the trumpet—' "

"Trumpet?" Uncle Lofton exclaimed. "You play a trumpet in church?"

"It's in the Bible!" Carl Mack said. "Look, it's God's word."

Uncle Lofton took the Bible and looked at it. He handed it to me. I read it and he watched me. When I was finished, he said, "Yeah, it's in the Bible!"

We handed the Bible back to him, and he read on.

" 'Praise him with harp and lyre. Praise him with the timbre and harp. Praise him with stringed instruments and organs—' "

When he said "stringed instruments," Carl Mack pointed to his guitar lying on the porch. "That's my guitar out there," he said.

Soon he and Carl Mack were singing a song. Then Mr. Roy Melvin got into it. They sang and played harp and guitar.

"That's what we need in the church round here!" Uncle Lofton said. "This ain't no church, but we can sing and play what we like!"

After they played and sang many songs, Mr. Roy Melvin and Buster Jacob went home, taking the footpath. Uncle Lofton asked Smilin' Henry and Carl Mack if they wanted to stay over for the night.

I decided I had to prepare myself for the snake's relatives when they came for me in the night. I'd get my lightning bugs. They would keep the room lit so that I could see the snakes when they came for me.

I went back into the room to get my jar of lightning bugs. Old man Spellman had told us if we crossed a lightning bug with a honeybee, we would get little honeybees who could make honey at night by using their lights as flashlights. He told us to collect them and bring them to him and he would cross them with honeybees. So I had a full jar.

I put my jar near my head on the pallet and fell asleep.

I woke up that Monday morning and realized that much to my surprise, the snakes hadn't come for me. I went into my bedroom and saw Carl Mack and Smilin' Henry just getting up. They had fixed their hair in stocking caps. They looked like old women.

"Good morning," Aunt Amanda greeted them in the dining room. "How'd you sleep?"

"Oh, just fine," Carl Mack said.

"And how did you sleep, Morris?" she asked.

"Okay," I said. I was so relieved that the snakes didn't get me that I wanted to yell for joy.

I sat down at the table for breakfast. I had solved the problem without Uncle Lofton's help and I felt proud that I had a firm grip on reality.

Chapter 9

When we got to the church for the crowning of the queen, we saw that a loudspeaker had been placed in front. The whole town could see where Jesus had taken up residence, Aunt Amanda said. Even Cherokee Indians and poor white trash couldn't resist the power of revival meetings. They came to the meetings and stood in the back.

I was sitting with Uncle Lofton in the deacon's section, the Amen Corner. To begin the ceremony, the Gospel Two did a concert. They started right out with a spiritual that was so sad and pitiful that I thought somebody had died. It was called "See How They Done My Lord." Moaning was the soul of black worship in our town, and Carl Mack and Smilin' Henry knew how to moan.

When Smilin' Henry slapped his hands on his leg that was the "hip-slapping style." And when Carl Mack stood with his legs apart and opened his mouth as wide as he could, that was the "flat-footed" style. They snapped their fingers and beat a tambourine. When Carl Mack sang in a deep voice, Smilin' Henry would sing in a high voice. They sounded like our dog Buckcaesar bellowing after a coon. Or maybe like a cat crying. Or maybe a screech owl we would hear in the woods at night.

When they finished, everybody was shouting in the aisle and falling over the benches. They were tearing the church up! As Daddy said, "These are hard shouters!" I watched Mrs. Cora Melvin's face as the Holy Ghost entered her. The Holy Ghost twisted her face into a frown that made her look like she was smelling a skunk, and her body jumped and she went down right beside Aunt

74

Amanda like somebody had hit her on the head with a hammer. Aunt Amanda picked her up on one arm and led her to the aisle where she began shouting again.

The whole church looked like a wagon train that a gang of Indians had jumped, killing everybody. People were hanging over the benches, exhausted. Others lay out in the aisle, holding their stomachs, or were lying on their backs kicking up their heels in the air.

A woman started talking in tongues in the back of the church. They held her by her arms. Her head was sunk down and rolled to the side, but her lips moved. The voice that came out of her lips sounded like the auctioneer at the tobacco market. Maybe it was the Lord. But the Lord is a holy man, so why would He want to speak through Sarah Jenkins, who was a little bit crazy anyway?

"They tore the church up!" Uncle Lofton said. He was right. They had *slaughtered* the church. When the excitement slackened, the people climbed back into their bench seats. To revive themselves, the Gospel Two sang a soothing song, and a calmness came over the people.

"Now we want to get down to the real business today," Smilin' Henry said.

"Yeah!"

"We want to see how much money Amanda Freeman has raised for the Gospel Two!"

"Yeah!"

"Praise the Lord!"

"In the other three churches, the highest amount of money raised for us was three hundred dollars. Now . . ." He turned to Mrs. Laura Melvin, who held a white envelope. "Now how much did Amanda Freeman raise?"

Laura Melvin came forth and opened the white envelope. "Amanda Freeman has raised five hundred and forty-six dollars and fifty cents!"

"How about that!" Smilin' Henry said. "Amanda Freeman is the queen!"

"Praise the Lord!"

"Hallelujah!"

Aunt Amanda smiled as she came to the center of the pulpit to receive her crown.

She had on one of those hats she brought back from the Smith's

Anchorage Club. It was green and had wings on each side. Inside the hatband it said, "Conceived in Paris."

Everybody watched as she took it off, glancing as she did at the shiny gold crown Smilin' Henry carried in his hand.

"I crown you the queen of Lee's Chapel," Smilin' Henry said, placing the crown of gold on her head.

Aunt Amanda bowed and said, "Thank you!"

Mr. John Smith was crowned king because he had raised more money than the other men. After they put his crown on his head, Smilin' Henry presented them with their gifts. Mr. John Smith got a Bible, and Aunt Amanda was given a picture of the Lord.

"I want to leave this picture here in the church," Aunt Amanda said, when she unwrapped the picture. "It belongs in the church. Look at it!" She raised the picture so everybody could see how pretty the Lord was.

He had golden blond hair and serene blue eyes. He was beautiful! But he looked white. Why was he white?

"Daddy, is the Lord a white man?" I whispered.

"Shut up!"

The whole church was clapping their hands, and the Gospel Two began to sing again, making everybody feel happy.

That night I opened a letter from my father in prison. Aunt Amanda wanted me to read it to her while she washed the dishes.

"What he say?" she asked.

". . . I hope the boys are fine. Tell Morris to be good, until I come home . . ."

"See! He is coming from prison soon!"

"When is he coming?"

Would we have to live with him? Wasn't he a mean man, and wouldn't he be mean to us?

"I don't know, it won't be long now," she said, her eyes looking at me thoughtfully. "Ain't you gonna be glad?"

Although I wanted him to come home, I didn't want him to take us away from Uncle Lofton and Aunt Amanda. They had been so good to us, and although I had promised my father I would be good, I wasn't sure he would be better to me than Uncle Lofton had been. My father was my hero, another bad nigger, but it would be better if he were still a long way away.

"No," I said. "I only want to be with you and Uncle Lofton."

"You'll like your daddy again, once you see him and y'all around him an git use to each other."

I didn't like the idea of his coming, but "soon" was an eternity away. I pushed it far into the back of my mind.

Chapter 10

〰〰〰〰〰〰〰〰〰〰

Summer 1952, age 9

One day Cornelius and I were playing when a white woman came into the yard and asked for Aunt Amanda. I ran inside and told her that a white woman was at the door. She asked me what kind of white woman, and I said, "The insurance woman!" Often white salesmen came to our door. There was the candy man, who left boxes of candy which Aunt Amanda sold to the tobacco hands at a few cents profit; there was the Bible man, who always managed to sell us a Bible. When white people came to our door, it was usually to sell something.

Aunt Amanda went outside to see the white woman.

"Sylvia!" she exclaimed, and ran outside to hug the woman. Who was she, then? From her clothes, her perfume, jewelry, and the car it was obvious that she was from the North.

"This is your Aunt Sylvia," Aunt Amanda said. "She is your mother's cousin. Go and hug her!"

"He couldn't remember me," the woman in the wide-brimmed hat said, looking down at me. "He wasn't but two years old. I used to carry him in the stroller."

She came toward me. Why did she want to kiss me? She looked surprised after I turned my cheek from her red lips.

"Don't you remember Sylvia?" Aunt Amanda asked.

It wasn't just that I didn't remember her—I didn't—but it was that she was white! My brother and I had never been that close to white people before, except our white playmates like Marge.

"Go on and kiss her!"

I obeyed Aunt Amanda and gave the woman a kiss, getting a whiff of perfume.

"Now isn't that sweet!"

"How's Cuffy?" she asked Aunt Amanda.

"We saw him," Aunt Amanda said. "He's doing fine. He writes all the time. He's a good Christian, says he prays every day." She looked down at me and my brother. "And he's just as crazy about his little yaller boys as he can be."

"And Dorothy?"

"She's up to Mrs. Commie's, as far as I know."

Aunt Sylvia straightened that large wide-brimmed hat with a gesture that I associated with black people who lived up north.

When Uncle Lofton heard about how we had mistaken Aunt Sylvia for a white woman, he was outraged. He said my brother and I were going to grow up so ignorant that we wouldn't even be able to recognize our own kin. To teach us about our relatives, he took us to visit my grandmother's people a few days after the arrival of Aunt Sylvia. He and Aunt Amanda had always taken us to visit our aunts and uncles and our cousins, which numbered in the twenties. But this visit was to our maternal grandmother's relatives.

"These are your mother's people," Uncle Lofton said as he drove into the yard of an old house. I watched an old man and woman who sat on the porch in a swing. Young children played in the yard. Beyond the house, in the background, stood a big white mansion with long white pillars. "They just a bout as sorry as your daddy's people."

"What is sorry people?" I asked him.

"Just no count people," he explained. "Boy, you got a lot to overcome in your family. I always told you that."

I had heard so much about how sorry my mother's people were that I was surprised to see that they were industrious people: behind the house was a big flourishing garden and tilled fields beyond that. I had expected them to be like my Grandma Commie's family in Bolton, my mother's people there, where everybody lay around in the sunshine, doing nothing, like in a Snuffy Smith cartoon.

Daddy stopped the Hudson and we got out. "Amanda and Lofton," the old man called out. "So good to see you!"

We walked up to the porch.

The old people looked down at me and my brother. "Now these is Dorothy and Cuffy's children!"

"That's right," Aunt Amanda said.

"Oh, they some big, nice boys," the old man said.

"This is your granduncle," Uncle Lofton said, introducing us to the old man and his woman. "John Hatcher and his wife. This is your grandmother's brother. Do you understand?"

I shook my head yes, but it didn't mean a thing to me. I kept my eyes on that big white house. I wanted to go and play around it. Perhaps I could find something like a marble.

"See that house yonder," he said, pointing to the big mansion. "Your grandmother was born right in that house." He took me by the shoulders and pointed me to a big tree at the back of the big white house. "See that tree?"

"Yes."

"Now that tree is the same tree that your great-grandparents swung on. They was slaves."

"That's right," the old lady rocking in the rocking chair said. "That's the tree they all plays under." Some children were playing under the tree. I could hear their shouting.

> "Little Sally Walker, sitting in a saucer,
>   Crying and sighing for some young man to come.
>   Rise, Sally, rise and wipe your weeping eyes."

A girl in a yellow straw hat danced in the center of the circle. I knew the game well. Now she turned to choose a lover. The boy she chose came into the circle with her. Now when they sang the last line he would kiss her.

> "Fly to the East and fly to the West,
>   And kiss the one you love best."

"Can we go and play with them?"

"No," Aunt Amanda said. "Stand here, and listen."

They talked in quiet whispers now, about our parents. They said it was tragic what had happened to my father and mother. What was it that my father had done? He was in prison, but why? Uncle Lofton would only tell us that we were too young to know. Therefore, it was difficult to understand why these relatives looked at us with sad looks and said, "Oh, it's terrible on the children!"

80

"This is Mrs. McNeil, a woman who cooked in the plantation for fifty years," Aunt Amanda told us.

Mrs. McNeil, a fat, squat old woman in a big apron, said, "It's true! John Hatcher know it's true! His mother, also yo great-grandmother, Dana Hatcher, was the daughter of Will Brown, the son of General Thomas Brown, who owned the Oakland Plantation that you see right over there!"

I gazed at it again.

"General Brown's father came to North Carolina in seventeen hundred and seventy-two and was given a tract of land from the king of England. That's how all of this mess got start. He fought against the Tories and won against them and built the plantation in eighteen hundred and thirty-two. The plantation was so well built that it still stands today! Look at it!"

The children ran back from the big tree toward the big house, filling the air with their laughter.

"Come on, Uncle John's gonna feed his peacocks!" his wife said. Because of his tender nature, Uncle John had a talent for raising peacocks, which were the pride of the plantation. We all moved from the porch to the fowl pen where he kept his peacocks.

Uncle John Hatcher was throwing feed to them. One of them spread his colorful tail feathers. "Uncle John and all of his people stayed on the plantation after the Yankee had come," Sylvia said. "They stayed on and took care of the plantation as they had many years before.

"Where is there to go?" said Dudley, Mrs. McNeil's husband.

After the peacocks had been fed and watched, we walked to the cemetery.

When we passed a tombstone, Mrs. McNeil would read out the name and date and tell us about them. "Your Grandmother Commie had two sisters," she said. "One was Lorene, who used to run a dance hall in Bolton, back in those days when Bolton had a dance hall. The other one was called Mary. She looked like a white woman. She was the purties gal in that whole bunch that come along with her."

We walked on a bit more and looked at other tombstones. I couldn't remember all the connections. The best I could make out was that my grandmother had two sisters and two brothers, Albert and John. The father of Commie, Mary, and John was a white man, one of General Brown's descendants.

81

"But these Browns are not the Browns you daddy come from," Uncle Lofton explained to us. "That's *another set* of Browns."

"Well, the people from your mother's side," Mrs. McNeil said, "weren't slaves. They was what you would call *Isshy* Negroes. Those were Negroes who had their freedom issued to them a long time ago. Your mother's people weren't slaves because they did the housework. They didn't work in the fields. No sir!"

"What about my father's people?" I asked. What *set* of Browns were those?

"Your father's people were the field hands. They worked all these lands you see here."

When we came back to the house, the old people sat on the porch again. The women brought out ice cream. When the ice cream was finished, we still wanted to go and play. This time we were allowed to go.

When released, we ran to the big tree. It was so large that it seemed to cover the entire sky. We ran to the back of the house and saw the slave quarters. Finding the path that led down to the Cape Fear River, we dashed down to the water's edge like our ancestors had many years before. At the end of the river, we saw large white magnolia trees and moss hanging down from the trees.

When we left there that night, my brother and I had a thousand questions. Hovering over the seat, we talked to Uncle Lofton and Aunt Amanda as we drove home. Did they beat the slaves? Why were the black people slaves? Where did the slaves come from? Africa! Where was it, Daddy! Way across the ocean where we all come from. Was Uncle John's daddy a slave?

Some weeks later, Uncle Lofton and Aunt Amanda took us to visit my father's people. They lived in a patch of woods on the other side of the Cape Fear River in a bend in the river called Carver's Creek. Would I discover why my real daddy was so bad?

As we drove into the dirt road, I looked out the window at the wilderness. There were very few houses, but when we did come upon one, it was filled with little black raggedy children. Savages! Were they savages like the ones I'd seen in the comic books?

"Uncle Lofton," I asked him as we drove up and the raggedy black kids stood in the yard gaping at us, "is this Africa?"

"No, this is where your Aunt Adelia lives."

I was afraid to get out of the car. When Aunt Amanda told us that these were our cousins, we ran away from them, because they were so dirty and ugly. It took a while before we relaxed enough to play with them.

Aunt Adelia was my father's oldest sister. She had a bunch of children and all the birthdays of all the Browns written in two Bibles. One of them belonged to her grandfather, Rich Brown.

She sat on the porch with the Bibles in her lap and told us about the family. Richmond Brown was the oldest member of the family who had actually been a slave.

The name Brown was the name he took, she said, when he came to the area. It was the name, she said, of his master, the man who brought him here. Before our name was Brown, she said, it was Flowers, and before that Daniel.

Great-Grandpapa Rich Brown was a medium-height man, brown skinned, with "open hair." He married a woman called Mitty, who was a schoolteacher, and had eleven children, three boys, eight girls. When he was freed as a slave, he worked in the turpentine business. When his wife died he married a young girl called "Yaller Cat" so that she could help take care of his daughter who was having a baby (the baby was Aunt Adelia herself). But while Rich was marrying Yaller Cat, he was "courting another woman down the road a piece."

While he was out one night, Aunt Adelia told us, Yaller Cat sneaked off herself and stayed in the hayloft. Rich Brown was so jealous that he stayed home the next night to keep her from going out. He stayed home to see what she was going to do. He thought she had been out that night with a man. So this is how she broke him, Aunt Adelia said, that was how women had to be to rule over men.

Aunt Adelia told us that Rich Brown, despite his big family, was an "orphan," an ex-slave who couldn't prove that he had a legal mother or father. Apparently, his fate changed after he arrived in Carver's Creek, where he bought a large tract of land and raised his family.

"That's the land he bought over there," Aunt Adelia said, pointing to the wide fields and trees.

We visited Mr. George Brown, the oldest Brown at that time. He was in his nineties. He was sitting in his swing as he told about our family.

"All these damn Browns kin to one another," he'd say. "There was a man who had a bunch of girls, eight, I believe. These eight girls married different men. Some was Beatties, some were Samsons. And all of these eight families had babies. That's how the Chord got started. They is all cousins all back up in there," he would say, waving his hand over the Chord, the small farm where my father grew up.

George Brown told us about Esau Brown, an early Brown ancestor—my great-great-grandfather—who revolted against his master and had to leave the plantation. We delighted in his Robinson Crusoe survival in the swamp where he had been forced to live with his wife, children, chickens, and pigs. George said, "He was so angry with the white man that he called himself an Indian."

Esau Brown was the first bad nigger, the prototype in our family. "Every black family had a 'bad nigger,'" George laughed. "Ours was Esau!"

"Why did they call 'em bad niggers?" I asked him.

"Cause that was *what* they was! Because that's how you *had* to be!" George said. "Now they had one that was worst than bad, he was uh *turrible* nigger. A black fellow called Slater, I believe. He shot and killed a policeman during an argument right up here in Bladen county and took off on a train. Now they had some others, too. Stagolee, and Dupree, and Railroad Bill, and a bunch mo."

He looked at Uncle Lofton and laughed, and then looked down at us. "Your granddaddy Cecil was purtty turrible, too. These was so mean times. The white folks said 'insolent Negro.' It was a nice way of saying 'bad nigger,'" Aunt Adelia said.

"These ones back up in here intimidated the whites, you know," George said. "On yo mother's side, you got the clever servant blood in yo, that Hatcher laughter and humor, but from yo father side, you got that insolent, rebellious, 'bad nigger'!"

Did he mean that something bad would happen to me, as it had to my father?

"Daddy, what do he mean?"

"He means that you and your brother will have to work hard to cover up all that meanness in your blood, that's what he means." But how could I do that if I didn't know what my father had done?

Later, when we were back home feeding up the animals, I asked Uncle Lofton again about Cuffy.

"What did he do, Daddy?"

"You have to ask him that, when he comes. It should be him that tell you."

I would do that, I would ask him what he had done, but it was going to be a long time before he came. From what George Brown said about Esau Brown, I realized that my father must have killed a white man. Didn't white people hate us because we were black? And wasn't my father a bad nigger? Would I too kill a white man one day? Would I go to prison? No, I would have to find a way to leave this town where the white people hated me because I was black. But how?

I asked Uncle Lofton about his life before and his life after he met Aunt Amanda. Compared to the other people in the village they were rich. They were married in 1936 and lived in a log cabin my grandfather Cecil built on a large tract of land he bought. In addition to farming tobacco, they ran an illegal whiskey still.

Daddy told me and Knee about the times when the high sheriff would drive down into the swamp looking for stills. He pulled up into the yard and while he and Uncle Lofton were talking friendly, one of Uncle Lofton's shoats that had been drinking in the mash staggered out from the yard.

"Lofton, what you reckon is wrong wit that pig?" the sheriff asked as the pig drunkenly collapsed at his feet.

"Oh, that ain't nothin. That's the cholera!" Uncle Lofton said.

"Cholera? Looks like that pig is drunk!"

"Oh, he is always like that. That's a peculiar pig," Uncle Lofton said loud enough for Aunt Amanda, who was in the back of the house loading the liquor into their brand-new 1942 Fleetwood Chevrolet, to hear.

"Lofton," the sheriff said, "let me take a look behind your house!"

"Now lemme tell yo something," Uncle Lofton said. "When that pohlessman started around the house, Aunt Amanda was backing the car around the other side of the house. While the pohlessmen was giving the pigs an alcoholic sobriety test, we got into that Fleetwood and took off!"

While he slopped the pigs or pitched hay to the white horse or fed the rabbits, or when we ran to meet him when he came off the railroad, Uncle Lofton would tell us about various legends of his family and that of my parents. These legends always illustrated how much respect, dignity, and courage our people had to have to endure the "meanness of white people"—the racism and hard times.

One of them was the legend about Uncle John, my mother's oldest brother, which we heard frequently. Once when we visited John Hatcher, I overheard Aunt Amanda, Uncle Lofton, Mrs. McNeil, and her husband Dudley talk about John.

"Oh, and you know what happened to John?" one of our relatives would begin. My brother and I would be present but not audible.

Aunt Amanda's head would lean over conspiratorially.

"No? What?"

"Well, you know he disappeared! Some said he is passing . . ."

"Now John was yo mamma's oldest brother," some older relative would remind us. "John's daddy was a white man. Doan nobody ever wanna talk about that, but he was."

"John had real good hair," Dudley said.

"Sort uh lak blond," Daddy said.

"That's right, that's right!" Dudley said. "Him and me come along ta gather."

"Me and him come up together, too," Uncle Lofton said. "But when he got up right good size, he went away from Bolton. He come back a few times, but every time only for a day or so and he would stay up there with Piggy Spann."

"Piggy Spann, Daddy, who is Piggy Spann?"

"Now you won't remember Piggy because Piggy been dead. Before you was born.

"Now in nineteen hundred and forty-two," Daddy went on, "the shipyard here at Wilmington was closing, but they was hiring up in Portsmouth, Virginia. Cline, my brother, John's brother, and Delmont Harvey went up there looking for work because that was where John was.

"He was gettin promotions in the shipyard because they thought he was white. He was going with them white gals too," Aunt Amanda said, adding another piece like she was laying a piece of cloth to a quilt they were all sewing.

"Well, they found out about him and got after him. He moved to a small town up in Virginia and nobody ever have heard from him again."

"He called Dorothy once," Aunt Amanda said. "When Cuffy got in trouble, cause he was crazy about Dotty and Cuffy."

86

"He got tired of being treated bad. He got tired of how they treated the colored, and by him looking like he looked, why he just passed!" Uncle Lofton said.

I often thought about how so many of my relatives suffered and how I would have to work hard to "overcome" (as Uncle Lofton described it) their fate. I thought of Uncle John passing for white. If I had a choice between the two, I'd do like Uncle John and leave Bolton and never come back. But if I stayed here, I'd have to be a bad nigger like my father or my great-great-grandfather, Esau Brown.

Chapter 11

During the summer of 1953, when I was ten years old, I discovered an enemy in white boys. My brother and our buddies Kenny and his brother Willie, whom we called Booty, and several other boys from Outback—Ruby Freeman, Leroy and Ernest Smith—would meet at the sawmill behind Mr. Crone's store and fight for possession of the top sawmill with another bunch of boys—boys from the white neighborhood in Bolton.

It all got started one late afternoon when Kenny asked me and my brother to go with him into Mr. Crone's store where he expected to sell soda bottles to Mr. Crone for two pennies each. As we hauled the bottles into Mr. Crone's store, we noticed three white boys hanging around the back of the store. One of them, Jimmy Harris, stood by his new bicycle. I looked at his blond hair and right into his blue eyes as I passed. If he bothered me I was going to hit him. I didn't like him. I wanted a bicycle, too.

When we came out, they were still there.

As they stood looking at us, we took offense and decided to beat them up. As we moved toward them, they moved back toward the sawdust pile. One of them climbed up the side of the sawdust pile, heading for the top. We started climbing on the other side, determined to take it before they got there.

When we got to the top, we were faced with the dirty-faced white boys. We stood staring at each other without saying a word. Suddenly I hauled off and hit the white boy in the face, knocking him back on the soil. His buddy was bigger, and he grabbed me and we tumbled down the sawdust. My brother and Kenny fought with the other two, and they also tumbled down the pile.

As soon as we got up from the bottom, we scrambled up the pile in an effort to regain the advantage. Again we met them eyeball-to-eyeball and punched each other in the face until we had managed to beat them down to the bottom of the hill.

When we came home that evening we had bloody noses and black eyes, but we were elated that we had beat the white boys up, and the news of our battle quickly spread among the other boys.

The next afternoon we went back to the sawmill and sure enough the white boys were there with an additional bunch of boys. Before we could make it to the sawmill, a white boy threw a rock that nearly hit Willie on the head. We grabbed rocks and started throwing them back.

Then Willie took out his slingshot, and fitting a rock in it, he pulled back the rubber and let go. We watched the rock find its mark on the white boy's thigh; the pain was so great that he went down in a frenzy. The other white boys grabbed him and pulled him to safety. Willie reloaded his slingshot and hit one of them again. They scrambled off back to the white neighborhood. We had won the battle because of Willie's slingshot.

As we went back home, we decided that we would all have to have slingshots. Booty would make them, but we had to supply the inner tube.

The next day, on the way home from church, we stopped by Grand Papa's house. Papa was a big man. He had worked in the woods all his life to make money to buy land in Bolton. Now he was in his sixties and lived alone in a house by the white people, next door to A. J. Harris.

My brother and I noticed that Papa Cecil wore a pair of rubber boots which he had cut along the tops. They looked like the kind of boots Robin Hood would wear, because the flap had been pulled down after he had cut away the top, which had been ruined.

"I want some boots like Papa," I said to Aunt Amanda, but she just pushed me away. If we got a pair of boots, we could cut them up to make slingshots.

"Boy, you better get out of my face," she said. "Yo always want something."

It wasn't but a few days later, Aunt Amanda took us to K. M. Holmes and bought us rubber boots. The next day, we sat down with scissors and cut the tops off the boots just the way Papa did his.

"Oh, my Lord, boy, what's happen to your boots!" Aunt Amanda demanded at dinner.

"We cut them like Papa's," my brother coolly announced.

"You cut up dem new boots?"

"Yes, ma'am, to look like Papa's."

Aunt Amanda couldn't believe it. She just collapsed in the chair and called Uncle Lofton from the yard.

"Lofton, look at that?"

"Boy, why did you do that?" Uncle Lofton asked, also subdued by shock. "You took those brand-new boots and cut them up. Why?"

"We like the way Papa's cut his boots and we wanted them to look like Papa's."

Uncle Lofton shook his head.

"What do you want to look like Papa's boots for?" Aunt Amanda asked.

"Like Robin Hood!" I ran to my room and got the comic book.

"Look! Just like Papa's boots!"

She looked at it and shook her head understandingly.

We delivered the rubber to Booty and he went into immediate production on the slingshots.

Mr. Buster sat on an orange crate near the door. His wife, Mrs. Minnie, sat on the big white porch with a few other women. Shebe, who was my age, and his other five brothers were scattered here and there between the shop and the porch.

"Good morning," Buster called out to Uncle Lofton as he came around the front of the car. Booty came by with a big knot on his head. He had been running from some white boys and ran into a chain on the railroad.

"Boy, what happened to your head?" his father, Mr. Roy Melvin, asked.

"Nothin," Booty told him.

"Now, you boys ain't out there fighting with them white boys, is you?" he asked.

"No sir," Booty lied, glancing over at me and Knee.

Uncle Lofton looked down at me. "My boys wouldn't ever do anything like that. These boys are pretty good." I felt terrible that I had deceived Uncle Lofton. What would he say if he knew that I was so bad?

"Crops doing real bad," Uncle Lofton said, returning to the subject he had introduced before Booty came up. "My bacco is wilting. Need rain, man."

"My crops is wilting, too," Buster said, taking the sodas from his son and handing them to me and my brother. "You think a new pastor is going to help?"

It was hot and dry in Bolton that Sunday. To keep cool, we all wore straw hats, even to church. I wanted to get away to talk to Willie to get all the details on what had happened.

"Daddy, can we go play?"

"No," Uncle Lofton said. "We got to go to the sermon in a few minutes." My brother and I exchanged an impatient look.

"Goin to see what that fellow Townsend's gone say?" Mr. Buster Smith asked Uncle Lofton. Elder Smith had been dismissed last Sunday because he couldn't preach. We were getting a new preacher and everybody wanted to see if he was worth keeping. But that wasn't of any interest to us young boys; we wanted to go find some white boys and have fun beating them up.

"He ain't called by God. He call his self."

"Don't say that," Aunt Amanda said, walking over to the porch where Mrs. Minnie raised her parasol to greet Aunt Amanda. "He's born right here in Bolton, just like the rest of us."

"But he call himself a preacher," Buster said, "and he wants to be the pastor of our flock. If God called him, that'd make him different from the rest of us. Suppose to, least it should."

"I don't care where he come up from," Uncle Lofton said. "If he is a good preacher, and he don't cut the Bible short, he alright."

"What y'all want?" Buster asked.

"Gib me a package of Lucky Strikes," Daddy said, "and let them boys drink a orange drink."

Buster turned his weight slowly to one of the boys sitting inside the store. "Gimme a drink for these boys and a package of cigarette," he said to Shebe, who moved slowly behind the counter.

"Something is wrong when a people without a pastor," Uncle Lofton said. "That last one wasn't worth two cents. He was after these women."

"Naw that ain't right, he wasn't after these women," Mrs. Minnie said. "These women wus after him!" Aunt Amanda laughed so loud I could see her gold tooth.

"Buddy, these women were crazy about that last preacher," she said. "I'm glad he's gone," Buster said. "Hell, I'd rather have no preacher than a no-good one."

"Yeah," Mrs. Minnie said. "But you know what they use to say. A cross-eyed man is the king in a world where everybody is blind. Wasn't nothin wrong with that preacher."

"Yeah there was," Uncle Lofton said. "He cut the Bible short."

As we passed through the swinging doors and into the sanctified air of the church and took our seats, I left Knee with Aunt Amanda and went with Uncle Lofton to sit with the men.

Buddy Townsend held up his hand for everybody to get quiet. When everybody had finally settled down, he approached the pulpit. Buddy Townsend spoke directly to the people.

I looked over the church at Aunt Amanda. A stout, round woman with a wide-brimmed hat and veil, she fluttered a fan in front of her face. My brother Knee sat beside her. He was still a baby, I thought, and not big enough like me to sit with the men in the deacon's corner, because they were real men who could pray.

I loved getting down on my knees like the men did and I loved praying with them—"Oh, Lord, Jesus in Heaven!"—putting my little voice right in there with their deep baritones. How thrilling it was for me to look up from my folded, praying arms and sneak peeks at the serious faces of the men. Those wrinkled black and brown faces looked to me just like saints, or what I imagined saints to look like. They had their eyes closed as in sleep, muttering prayers to Jesus, just like they were playing hide-and-go-seek.

Then, I'd look across the whole church. I'd stick my head up to see if everybody was praying. Sometimes I'd see my brother's head sticking up. I would look at Aunt Amanda and the women sitting by themselves.

After prayer was over, I looked out the window. The crop was wilting in the hot sun. If the preacher was any good, I could hear Uncle Lofton saying, he would bring us some rain. That would mean that the Lord favored us.

In front of us the new pastor was taking his place behind the pulpit and preparing himself to give his virgin sermon. If they didn't like him, he would have to go.

"Let the church say Amen," he said, in a soft voice.

"Amen!"

"Let the church say Amen—again!"

"Amen!"

"Yes, sir!"

"A-men!"

"Preach! Preach!"

"I just want to say to you how very . . . happy! . . . I am to be with you . . . this morning!"

"Thank you, Jesus!"

"And . . . I just want to say . . . it's a blessing to be here with you this first Sunday in August and to tell you how happy I am to have Carl Mack and Smilin' Henry praising the Lord with us in song!"

The church went mad with excitement.

He moved back from the pulpit, a signal that he was about to enter into the first part of his sermon—the part where he would give the text: "We want to say a few words in behalf of our Lord and Jesus—"

"Yeah—"

"Want to say a few words from the gospel as recorded by St. Matthew fourteen chapter and thirty-first verse for our text this morning." He leaned over the Bible and read, "And immediately Jesus sat forth his hand and caught him and said unto him, 'Wherefore did thou doubt?'—"

"Uh-huh!" moaned the church.

"And we chose for a subject this morning, a disciple with little faith."

"Uh-huh."

"Because we all are disciples for the Lord."

"Yeah!"

"And to determine how much faith we have is when we get caught in a situation—"

"Yeah—"

"Uh-huhhhh!"

". . . that we don't know how to get out of. Let us pray," he said, and leaned on the pulpit. The elders got down on their knees and so did I.

"Father God in the name of Jesus, we are calling on your Name right now."

"Yeah—"

"—Oh, Lord, if you will, please, Sir, have *Mercy* on *your* people here this morning—"

"—Yeah."

"—Please come down and move me, move self, Lord, out of the way, that Thou might come and manifest yourself, that the person of your Holy Spirit might be seen here in First Born Church this morning—"

"—Oh yes!"

"—Because, Lord, we need you—right now!—"

"—Yes, Jesus—"

"Like we never needed you before—"

"Yes, Lord—"

"—Speak to us, Lord God . . ."

"Yes!—"

"That some things on your mind might be confined to the soul of your people, this we ask in Jesus' name—Amen!"

"Amen!"

He leaned back and repeated his text. "A disciple with little faith! Now we all know what faith is, because in Hebrew two, chapter one it says faith is things hoped for and evidence of things not seen."

"Yeah!"

"So we know now what faith really is!"

"Oh yes!"

". . . But Jesus said to one of his disciples, 'Oh, Thou of little faith!' "

"Yeah!"

"And we find from time to time, we are faced with little faith!"

"Yeah!"

"When sickness comes in our home!"

"Yeah!"

"When the newborn baby takes a turn for the worse . . ."

"Yeah!"

"Or . . . or . . . when there is no food on the table . . ."

"Yeah!"

". . . Then we find that our faith is not what we thought it was!"

"Preach it, preach it!"

"When death comes into your home, when mother or father, or brother or sister are called Home to Rest . . ."

"Oh, Jesus!"

94

". . . But Peh-tur . . . You know the story about Peter—Peh-tur, you know, had seen Jesus earlier . . . walking on Wahtar, and you see, man had never walked on Wahtar before. Peh-tur was on a ship, you know, and Peh-tur sort of looked over the side of the ship and here come a *Man* . . . with a halo around His head . . . a Man walking on the Wahtar . . . just as though He walked on dray land."

"Yeah."

"And Peh-tur *began to fasten his eyes upon Jesus."*

"Yeah—"

I thought of the only lake I knew—Lake Waccamaw where Aunt Amanda went to work at the Smith's Anchorage Club. I imagined Jesus walking on that lake and I imagined Buddy Townsend as Jesus.

"And Peh-tur turned to the others on the ship and said, 'Ooooohhh, look, what I see coming!' and they all began to cry out, 'Is this a ghost, or is this a spirit that we see coming?' "

"Uh-huh."

"And as Jesus came near—"

"Uh-huh."

"Got closer to the ship—"

"Uh-huh—"

"And Peh-tur merely stepped off the ship—"

"Yeah."

"—Oh, if you let me reminisce a minute now—" Buddy Townsend then threw his head back and placed the back of his fist on his forehead.

"Go ahead!"

"I see Peh-tur now . . ." he said, and with his eyes closed, he told us about the picture we couldn't see. "I see Peh-tur as he stepped with his sandal off the ship and I see his sandal as it gathers Wahtar . . . and I see Peh-tur as he stepped off the side of the ship. But he keeps his eyes on Jesus!"

I pictured Peter, too. He looked, with all that woolly hair, like Uncle Lindsey.

"What out now!"

"And as long as Peh-tur kept his eyes on Jesus everything was alright."

"Yes!"

"And Peh-tur kept on stepping—Jesus said if you make one

step, I'll make two steps, and Peh-tur was worrisome about his fourth step. And Peter took another step and kept his eyes on Jesus, but you know there is something about the same Wahtar that Peh-tur was walking on, and he had made the fourth step. And what happened to Peh-tur then is something that happens to all of us. You see the Lord tells us to come unto me, and when we step out of our way in going to Jesus, we take our eyes off the Master—"

"Oh yeah!"

"—And Peh-tur took his eyes off the master and he began to step down into the Wahtar, that same Wahtar he had walked on . . . that same Wahtar he had seen the master walk on—"

"Step on the gas!"

"He opened his mouth to drink up the water—"

"Uh-huh—"

"—But you know an amazing thing happened then—"

"Yes suh!"

"As he began to sink down into the Wahtar, Peh-tur remembered what the savior had said, 'Oh, thou of little faith,' and then Peh-tur was going down into the water—"

I sat there mesmerized by the power of the image of Jesus and "Peh-tur," and I could see it so clearly. But what I liked so much was the way that Peh-tur and Jesus talked to each other.

Now Buddy Townsend began to speak in short, rhythmic sentences; and he began to move more rapidly from one side of the pulpit to the other. Then he reached up and took out the white handkerchief and began to wipe the sweat from his brow. This was the signal that he was about to "get down," as the people said, and preach. This was my favorite part of the sermon, "the pull."

"And I heard, hah!, the master said to Peh-tur, hah!, a little faith, hah!, is better than no faith, hah!, and church, hah!, I want to say, hah!, if you have, hah!, no faith, hah!, you ought to come, hah!, to Jesus!, just as you are, hah!, because if you have no faith, hah!, you gonna get in trouble, hah!, and then Peh-tur, hah!, realized, hah!, that he had been with God, hah!, that had walked the Wahtar, hah!, that Jesus told him to do, hah!, but then Peh-tur, hah!, he realized, hah!, that all faith, hah!, is possible with God, hah!, if you have trouble in your home this morning, if you got trouble in the hospital this morning, hah!, if you got trouble with another church, hah!, you ought out lean to God, hah!, because a little faith is better than no faith at all, hah!"

He went on like this for another half hour.

Making yet another shift, Buddy Townsend ended in a soft, normal voice, saying, "Let the choir sing!"

Immediately the church choir and Gospel Two started swinging with, "Walk with Jesus!"

People started shouting again.

"Lord God, let all of those people who want to come to the moaning bench, do so right now! Right now!" This was the part in the service when he would save souls, and that's what he started doing.

Everybody started rushing to the pulpit, and a line was formed as he reached out his hand to touch one woman. Piggy Spann's wife, Mrs. Alberta, jumped when he put his hand on her head just like she had been hit with a bolt of lightning.

"Touch them, Lord! Touch!" Buddy Townsend cried out, as he laid his hand on somebody's head. You could literally see Jesus come into them, at least I could see Him coming into them.

The deacons in the Amen Corner shouted, "Elder Townsend! He is Elder Townsend!"

"He ain't Buddy Townsend any mo," Daddy moaned beside me. "He is Elder Townsend now!"

"Yes, Elder Townsend," the others yelled, followed by the whole church. "Elder Townsend!"

Buddy turned to them and bowed, like he was thanking them for making him into Elder Townsend.

People were fainting all over the church. When the shouting died down, we realized that it had been thundering outside. The shouting was so loud that nobody paid much attention to anything else.

Elder Townsend heard the thunder, though.

"The Lord Gawd has answered our most precious of prayers!" he shouted, walking from the pulpit to the edge of the church. "Listen!"

The church grew quiet. What was it? Outside the window the clear sky began to get dark. Then Mrs. Suzanne opened the doors, and Cleo Bowen ran outside. Others followed. Soon I was running outside too.

Cars had stopped on the road to hear the music and the shouting.

A big clap of thunder rolled out of the sky as we walked out of the church.

Uncle Lofton stopped and looked up.

The sky turned dark blue, and yellow lightning cracked, and sent a blue streak across the fields in the distance. Then suddenly water from the sky fell into the churchyard like somebody in heaven had emptied a pail of it on our little dry church.

"Jesus Walked the Water!" somebody bellowed out.

"Ye of Little Faith!"

". . . Wahter! Wahter! . . ."

It was raining . . . Yes, it was. And Buddy Townsend had become Elder Townsend.

When we got in the car, I leaned across the seat to Uncle Lofton.

"Daddy, why did the people like our church so much?"

"Because God was there."

"Oh, yes he was!" Aunt Amanda exclaimed exuberantly.

"Why was he there?"

"He wanted to answer the prayers," Uncle Lofton told me.

"If anybody pray to God for something will he give it to them?"

"Yes, if you pray for something that you really want bad enough."

"Don't forget to say your prayers," Uncle Lofton told me just as we were going to bed. Smilin' Henry and Carl Mack had found better accommodations since their sudden success in our town. Now, Knee and I could have our room to ourselves again.

As I kneeled beside the bed I thought about that bicycle I wanted. I remembered how Elder Townsend had prayed, so I folded my hands and began, "Oh, God, hah!, will you, hah!, bring me that, hah!, little red bicycle, hah!, . . . But Peh-tur . . . You know the story about Peter. Peh-tur, you know, had seen Jesus earlier . . . walking on Wahtar, and you see, man had never walked on Wahtar before. Peh-tur was on a ship, you know, and Peh-tur sort of looked over the side of the ship and here come a *Man* . . . with a Halo around His head . . . a man walking on the Wahtar . . . Just as though He was walkin' on dry land!"

"Son, what are you doing?"

I looked up and saw Uncle Lofton standing over me.

"I'm praying," I said. "Like Elder Townsend."

"Why are you praying for a bicycle?"

"Because that's what I want. Jimmy Harris got one. I want one like he got."

"Jimmy Harris?"

"Yes, he got one."

"But why do you pray to God for one?"

"Because Elder Townsend said, 'Keep your eyes on Jesus and everything will be alright.' So I was praying and keeping my eyes on Jesus. If I pray for a bike will Jesus give it to me? He will, won't he?"

He looked up at Aunt Amanda, who stood in the door now.

"The Lord can't bring you a bicycle just like that," she said, glancing at Uncle Lofton. "But if you *work* a little for it, the Lord will help you get a bicycle. Ain't that right, Lofton?"

"That's right. You have to work a little for it. And pray at the same time."

"But you said I should pray for it, and he will give it to me."

"You have to do something to help Jesus give it to you."

"But why did he give one to Jimmy?"

"Jimmy's daddy owns a store. And Jimmy's daddy is the boss on the railroad. Jimmy's daddy is a white man and I ain't white."

"That means I can't get a bicycle?"

"You can get a bicycle but—" He thought about it and then he said, "Yes, you can get a bicycle. But you have to do it this way. You have to pray a bit and you have to work a lot—like wash the kitchen floor every Saturday for twelve Saturdays."

That made sense to me. I knew that Uncle Lofton and Aunt Amanda were good for their word, so for the next twelve Saturdays I washed the kitchen floor and left it sparkling and shiny. On the last Saturday, I went into the living room and saw Aunt Amanda pulling the cardboard off a red bicycle.

It was bigger than me, and I couldn't ride it. I had to push it along and jump on the pedal and ride it like a scooter. I let the big boys talk me into letting them ride it. Booty Melvin took advantage and rode it all the way to A. J. Harris's and back. I was crying when he gave it back to me, for I feared he had broken it. When I got it back, I promised myself I would learn to ride it.

Eventually, I rode it to A. J. Harris's myself. I saw Jimmy standing by the store with his bicycle. I realized then that his bike was a trainer-bike and mine was an adult-style bike, a much nicer bike. Seizing on this advantage, I went up to him to show off my new acquisition.

"How did you get a bike?" he asked me.

"Just like you did," I said. "I prayed for it."

"Prayed for it?" he asked, astonished. "I never prayed for a bike."

It figured too, considering the kind of bike he got. My bicycle was bigger, and prettier, and newer.

"If you'd prayed for it," I said, thinking quickly, "you would have gotten a bigger one."

To show off for Marge, who had ambled up to us, I started preaching like I'd seen Elder Townsend do.

"But why did you have to pray for one?" Jimmy wanted to know.

"So that I didn't have to get Booty to make a slingshot to hit you upside yo head and take yours!" I said, hopping on my bike and riding gleefully away.

Chapter 12

〜〜〜〜〜〜〜〜〜〜〜〜〜〜〜〜〜〜

Fall 1954, age 11

Uncle Lofton said, stepping into the hog pen, "And I didn't know it!"

"Don't think the Lord looked down on you, Lofton," Mr. Buster said, sharpening the knife. "None of us knowed Elder Townsend was a called man, called by the Lord to preach to us."

My brother and I stood a safe distance away. We wanted to see how they killed the hog but we were afraid to look. We were able to see Uncle Lofton swing the ax and hear the hog squeak. Then, Mr. Buster jumped across the wire fence and cut his throat. Soon they would be yelling for pans to put the guts in.

We went closer now that the men had stopped talking. They dragged the hog out by his hoofs onto a board. Then the hog was lifted up and they put his head into the barrel of boiling water that had been buried into a ditch bank. To keep the water hot, it had to be replenished from a boiling washing pot.

My brother and I had the job of keeping the fire under the washing pot blazing. We had to take the hot water from the washing pot to the barrels.

"Here! Here! Pour me some water here!" Uncle Lofton demanded, and I lifted the hot bucket of water up and poured it on the hairy body of the dead pig.

As the hot water scalded the skin, Uncle Lofton pulled the hair off the hog, leaving a white skin. While he worked, spinning the hog over and scraping off the wiry hair, Uncle Lofton talked more about Elder Townsend. After they hung the hog up by his hamstrings, they took out his guts, which we had to take to the house in a pan. Aunt Amanda and Mrs. Suzanne cleaned guts for chitlins. They ground the meat into sausages, packing it into skeins that were thrown across the clothesline to dry.

After the hog was cut up, Daddy would salt it down for nine days, a process which would dry it out and keep it from rotting. Then he would spread a mixture of black pepper and molasses on it and smoke it in the smokehouse every other day.

As I brought some meat into the kitchen, I noticed from the rise and fall of their voices that Aunt Amanda and her friend Mrs. Bowen were discussing something of grave importance. I paid enough attention to learn that it had something to do with her job as a cook at the Smith's Anchorage Club on Lake Waccamaw.

"The Smiths got a new bowling alley, Miz Suzanne. And it's something nice!"

Mrs. Betty, Reverend Bowen's wife, was there helping with the sausage too.

"Yes, it's so nice!" she said. She also worked with Aunt Amanda as a cook.

"They gettin ready to hire a bunch of boys to work in that bowling alley, setting up pins."

"My Felton is working there already," Mrs. Betty said. "Manda got him that job."

"That boy makes a lot of money," Aunt Amanda said. "I have seen the white people just give him money. Big old handfuls of money."

I loved the idea of making money since picking cotton, star grass and getting my bike by scrubbing the floor every Saturday. Now I saw the chance to earn some more money.

"Aunt Amanda," I said, putting the plate on the table, "I want to work some more and make money."

Aunt Amanda turned to me.

"You want to do what, honey?"

"I want to work," I said.

She smiled at her friends and pulled me to her. "You want to make some money?" Aunt Amanda loved working. She picked cotton, hoed corn, cooked pies, washed dishes with an impressive energy and pleasure. She enjoyed hearing that I wanted to work with her at the Anchorage Club.

"Yes. I want me some money!"

"Well, you too young to work setting up pins. But I can train you to help me set up the tables. Alright?"

"Okay," I agreed. "When do we start?"

"When you want to start?" she asked.

"Now!"

"Okay, you come with me to work tomorrow!" Aunt Amanda said, laughing. "You and you little brother!"

I was delighted. I had always been curious about the Smith's Anchorage Club. It was a mystery to me. All I knew was that after we had finished eating, she would disappear into their bedroom and reappear a few minutes later in her starched white uniform, complete with a white cap, and white hospital shoes. She looked like a nurse.

I knew she worked for white people, but I didn't have a mental picture to go with the idea. Once she had taken us there, and I vaguely remembered a huge white building, like a castle, and the blue water that was in front of it. I remembered, also, many white people. I was interested in white people because they were regarded by all the black people I knew as being different from us. Beyond my adventures with Marge, a little white girl I played with one summer, I had no way of learning anything about them. Now I would enter their world where Aunt Amanda would train us as waiters.

Outside the window of our car, the cypress trees heavy with gray moss slipped by. Beyond them I could see the steel-blue water of Lake Waccamaw. Between the cypress trees and the water I could see big boats. Yachts. Sailboats. Somebody was waterskiing. White people and water sports. They were rich and strange to me.

Aunt Amanda pulled the car up into the gravel road of the Smith's Anchorage Club, a big white building with many rooms.

When we got out a little old white lady met us.

"Amanda," she said, "are these your children?"

"No, Mrs. Smith," Amanda said. "These are my brother's boys."

"Well, they sure are cute."

"Thank you."

"Are they going to help out?"

"Yes, I'm going to train them," Aunt Amanda said.

103

"Well, that's nice."

She trained us to bring in the firewood and to set the table.

"Now when you bring the firewood in," she said, pointing to the big box near the fireplace, "don't throw it down, Morris. Put it down gently."

"Yes, ma'am."

"And don't let your brother throw it down either!"

"Okay."

We went out to the woodpile and brought in the first load. We entered the large room where the fireplace was and I gently eased my armload down. But Cornelius threw his down, creating a loud sound.

"He did it!" I said.

"But you are the oldest and I told you not to let him do it!" Aunt Amanda said.

I didn't like that arrangement. I was told to keep my brother in line because I was the oldest, but how could I tell him what to do? He never listened to me anyway.

Our next chore was to set the table, and Aunt Amanda showed us how.

"No, don't put the forks in the plate," she said, standing over us, watching. "Put the forks beside the plate."

Noticing that I did it correctly, she said, "Very good, Morris. Now I want you boys to finish up with this and bring out the water and pour each glass full.

We filled the glasses and went back to the kitchen. The whole place was in an uproar. The cooks were running from stove to stove. Fumes seemed to be shooting up all over the place.

"You boys come here," Aunt Amanda said, taking us to another room. There were some drinks on a table.

"Now, you see that man sitting by the fireplace?" she asked me.

"Uh-huh!"

"That's Mr. Johnson!" she said. "He is the president of the bank!" She took us by the hand and introduced us. Like all of the white people in this club, Mr. Johnson was delighted with Aunt Amanda and her two little children. She went around and introduced us to all of the important white people of Whiteville.

I soon began to see what a powerful position Aunt Amanda played in the life of the Anchorage Club. She was chief of the kitchen staff and had a group of blacks working for her. These were people from Outback, all good friends of hers. She hired them, picked them up for work, drove them to the club, and took them home.

I noticed a man who seemed different from the rest. He was dressed in white and was very distinguished. "Aunt Manda! Who is that?"

"Don'cha know who that is? That's Dr. Dawson. Now, he is the man who brought you into this world," Aunt Amanda said. "I want you to take him his drink and don't spill a drop."

"Aunt Amanda, how did he bring me into the world?"

"He delivered you! He was the doctor who spanked you and gave you your first breath of life!"

"And me too?" Knee wanted to know.

"No, not you! You were born in Portsmouth, Virginia, in a hospital. But Morris was born right there in his Gramma Commie's house!"

I looked closer at the man. I vaguely remembered that when Uncle Lofton's grandmother was very sick, Dr. Dawson came in his black Ford with his little black bag and sat on her bed and put something in his ear and then put a tube on her chest. But until this time, I never knew that he had the distinction of having delivered me into the world.

Now I saw a way to return to him the gratitude.

"Now, go on and take him that drink!" I took the drink up in the tray and started toward him.

"Now watch him!" Aunt Amanda said from the kitchen. Mrs. Smith looked on, as did Mrs. Betty, who stood behind Aunt Amanda. I walked between the tables being careful not to stumble into anybody.

I brought the drink up to Dr. Dawson, who sat there staring at the fire. He was not so old, but his hands trembled when I handed him the drink.

"Thank you, young man!" he said, smiling at me. His white suit dazzled me as if he were a god covered in some heavenly robe.

"You welcome," I said.

I stood there hoping for some opportunity to impress him. He seemed so aloof that I was a bit afraid of him.

Finally, I dashed off back to the kitchen.

"What did he say?" Aunt Amanda asked me.

"Nothing."

105

"Did he ask you whose boy you was?"

"Uh-uh!"

"Oh, Dr. Dawson is peculiar, that's all!" she said, shaking her head. "Y'all ready to eat something?"

"Yes, ma'am."

She took us to another room where some of the kitchen help was sitting at a table.

She came back with two plates filled to with food. We started right in. It was the same kind of food she brought home with her every night. She brought us two big glasses of milk and went off.

When Aunt Amanda announced that we were going to sing for everybody, we were led into the big room and placed in front of the huge fireplace. We sang the songs and got applause and tips and candy with a sticky texture that made me think of old white ladies.

While we were singing, I looked over at Dr. Dawson to see if he was watching. I tried to imagine him pulling me out of my mother and spanking life into me. Later, I asked Aunt Amanda for the details of my birth, and she told me how I was born in my grandmother's house. I had seen the house and knew the room. I was a big baby—nine and a half pounds.

A few Sundays later, after church, my foot fell asleep and refused to wake up. I went around hopping on one foot for several days, until Daddy asked me what was wrong. I didn't know, so he decided to take me to Dr. Dawson.

I was delighted when we drove to Lake Waccamaw. I was more excited by the fantasy of seeing a doctor in his office with all of his equipment than I was concerned about my foot. Daddy dropped me off and told me he would be back to pick me up in an hour.

I went into the clean white office and told the nurse who I was and that I wanted to see the doctor. When I went into Dr. Dawson's office, he asked me to show my foot to him.

"Doctors don't know everything," he said. "Why does your foot limp suddenly? Sometimes you can look at the symptoms and detect the reason. When did you discover that your foot was asleep?"

I remembered that when I came out of the church I was limping.

"Sunday?"

"Yes, sir."

"Was it a long sermon?"

"Yessir!"

"Who was preaching?"

"Elder Townsend!"

"Oh, that young black tobacco hand who transformed himself into Elder Townsend. It amazes me to see this transformation, just as it amazes me to hear the stories of these clever con artists! Tell me, did you sit with your legs crossed?"

"Yessir!"

"How did you sit? Which way did you put your legs?"

I showed him how I sat.

"You could have cut off the blood in your circulation."

Then he took out a book. After a few minutes of flipping through it, he looked up at me.

"Do you want to read what the possibilities are?" he said, and shoved the book to me.

I leaned over it and looked at the print. Was it possible that he didn't know? A young white woman came into the office.

"Oh, Doctor, I didn't realize that you were with somebody?"

"Oh, that's alright, Mildred. I'll be right with you! Go on in my office."

Dr. Dawson turned back to me. "Read through that book and find out what's wrong with you. I'll be back in a little while." He disappeared in the room with the white lady.

I flipped through this book and wondered about white people and medicine. Did white people have medical knowledge in their heads? Or was knowledge in books for all people?

I was so engrossed in reading the book that I didn't hear Dr. Dawson when he came back.

"Well, tell me, sir? What's the patient's diagnosis?"

"I don't know," I said, embarrassed. I wanted to ask him if I could be a doctor if I studied, but I was afraid. Was a white man like Dr. Dawson born a doctor or did he study books and learn to be a doctor?

"What did it say in the book?" he asked, pointing to the print.

I read out what was printed about circulation.

"Do you think that could have happened to you?"

"I don't know."

"Well, wiggle your foot!"

I wiggled my foot.

"Try to walk!"

I put my foot down and stood up, and walked.

"You're okay." He laughed. How could I thank him? How could I tell him that I knew he had brought me into the world? I turned to the door and went out.

I was excited to tell Daddy that I wanted to be a doctor as I waited for him to pick me up. I was fascinated by the idea that knowledge was in a book and that even I could learn to be a doctor.

Chapter 13

~~~~~~

Fall 1955, age 12

"**I** got me a job," Sidney Bowen said, as we walked home from the playground.

"Where?"

"At Smith's Anchorage. Setting up pins."

"That's what I wanna do." I remembered my old ambition. Now I was old enough to do it, I thought to myself.

"Your Aunt Amanda got me the job."

"I work at the Anchorage too," I told him.

"Yeah, what you do?"

"We're taking in the wood and stuff like that. And singing."

"Singing? How much you get?"

"A lot."

"How much?"

"Twenty dollars," I lied, and watched his eyes get big. I was always lying just to see how people would get excited. It was like telling the girls dirty words.

"God-lee! Twenty dollars. What you gonna do with it?"

"Saving it."

"For what?"

"Going to take a trip to see my father. In New York."

It went on like this, me lying and him believing every word of it until he said, "Did you see Mrs. Smith's poll parrot?"

"No. Where?"

"They got this poll parrot that can say 'Nigger.' "

"What else can he say?"

"He can say a lot of things."

"Like what?"

"He can call your name."

"Can he call 'Morris'?"

"Yeah," he said, turning down to the path that led to their house.

Later, when Knee and I were finished at the Anchorage Club, we went over to the bowling alley. The white people were bowling and there were five black boys at the other end setting up the pins after they were knocked down. The white people would laugh and drink and cuss when they missed knocking down the pins. The black boys just stood there solemn and silent. Whenever a pin was knocked down, they rushed over and put it up again.

We asked Aunt Amanda how much these boys got to set up pins.

"Sometimes five dollars a night!"

"Can I do that?"

"Boy, you crazy? You too young for that. Now here is what I want you to do," she said, leading us upstairs. She clicked on a light and we saw that we were in the attic.

She pointed to a hole in the ceiling and said, "When I tell you to, take these scissors and cut this string and the balloons will fall down. This mayor of Whiteville is giving a party for his friends and we want the balloons to fall on the party. Okay?"

She gave me the scissors and showed me the string.

"Knee, you hold the string so Morris can cut it," she said, "and I'll go downstairs!"

She went downstairs and we waited. We got down on our knees and looked through the hole at the white people.

"We can spit at them," Knee said.

"Don't do that. We'll get in trouble."

He did it anyway. He spat down on the crowd of white people, but nobody looked up.

"I hate them!"

"Don't do that!!!"

He took his penis out and held it over the hole.

"Don't do that!"

But I wanted to pee on them too. I didn't know why, but I wished I could pee on them and see what would happen.

110

Before I could stop him, I saw piss shooting down the hole.

"Hey, man, we gonna get a beating!"

But he was laughing and peeing. So I cut the string and let the balloons fall. I jumped up and ran for the door. Knee came behind me. We met Aunt Amanda on the way down the stairs.

"We did it!"

"It was too soon! But that's okay," she said.

She came out of the kitchen with me and Knee. Balloons were everywhere and floating over the room. An old white woman ran up to Aunt Amanda.

"Mandy, could you please get me something to wipe this champagne off me. Somebody was throwing water or champagne all over me!"

"Oh, just a minute, Mrs. Jordan!" Aunt Amanda said, and rushed off to the kitchen.

The woman looked down at us and smiled.

"Such nice boys," she said, taking the cloth from Aunt Amanda.

When she left, Knee and I laughed. We felt we had gotten away with murder. Why did I hate these white people and feel good about insulting them? Why did they treat us so differently from how they treated themselves?

A tall, old, wrinkled man, Mr. Smith, came up to us.

"Little boys," he said, "could you please go and bring in some more wood."

It was about eleven o'clock and cold outside. We didn't want to go but we knew that we would have to. "Could you please do it now. Thank you!"

"You ass, sir!" Knee said, but he said it in such a way that if you weren't listening closely it would sound like "yessir!"

"Thank you!"

We went to the woodpile laughing our heads off. We knew that we had to do what he wanted us to do, but the fact that he was too stupid to know or hear that we were also calling him an ass gave us satisfaction.

From that moment on it became a delight to take orders from Mr. Smith.

After dinner, Aunt Amanda brought out our guitars and said, "Mr. Smith wants you to sing a song."

We went in front of the fireplace where a hundred people stood around. We sang "I Heard Music Just Above My Head!" We were a big hit and then we did another song, a spiritual which we had learned from Smilin' Henry and Carl Mack.

The white people gave us money for the songs or some of them would give the money to Aunt Amanda.

"These boys were so good, Amanda," I heard one woman tell her. "They should be in show business."

"Thank you," Aunt Amanda said.

When we went home that evening we had collected five dollars each in tips.

"Aunt Amanda," I said, not being able to wait, "do Mrs. Smith have a poll parrot?"

"Yeah she got one. Why you wanna know?"

"Can he talk?"

"Oh, that thing can talk and says the nastiest things too. He got a mouth worse than you."

"Next time we go to the Anchorage can I see him?"

"I reckon so."

I went outside and found Elmo with one of his buddies, June Bug, sitting on the fence of the bull pen. Uncle Lofton had a big black bull called Fred who he used to breed the cows with. It was a favorite place to sit because the fence around the pen was very sturdy. They were smoking cigarettes.

"Hey, boy," Elmo said,

"Hey, Elmo, Mrs. Smith got a poll parrot that can say nigger."

He and June Bug laughed.

June Bug said, "He better not call me nigger or I'll kill him! I'll take that motherfucker and wring his neck, like this woman did that had one who use to fuck her chickens!"

"Say what? He used to fuck the chickens?" he laughed.

"They say the Blue sisters had a poll parrot that kept fucking the chickens and she told the poll parrot, say, 'Look, you fuck my chickens one mo time, and I'm gonna cut your hair off.' So the next time he fucked the chicken, she cut his hair off. All of it. He was bald headed as Piggy Spann was. So she took the parrot to church. And two deacons in the church was bald headed. So they come in the church and sat down. You know, like they sit down up front. And the poll parrot was sitting down in the back. Way in the back.

"So come time for the sermon, and the poll parrot leaned over and said, 'Hey, you two bald-headed chicken-fuckers, come on back here and sit by me!"

112

"What else did the poll parrot say?" I asked.

"Did you hear the one about the zebra," Elmo said, looking over at the big black bull. "This zebra came through with the circus, but she broke out and started wandering all across Bolton. She come to a farm and saw the little ducks. She said, 'What do you do?' Duck say, 'I go quack! quack! I'm a duck!' So she went on till she come to the pig. She say, 'What you do?' He said, 'I am a pig! I go root! root! root! They kill me and make sausage.' So she goes on and comes to the bull. She said, 'What do you do?' The bull said, 'You take off them striped pajamas and I'll show you what I do!'"

"Tell some more about Polly!" I said.

"This man," June Bug said, "had a pet store and a nigger went in there to buy a pet for his wife. He told the fellow, said, 'I want an unusual pet.' So the guy said, 'We got a monkey over here.' The man said, 'That ain't unusual enough.' Say, 'We got a goldfish.' Man said, 'That ain't unusual enough!' So he saw this parrot over there wearing glasses, reading a newspaper, smoking a pipe. So the guy said, 'What about him? He looks pretty unusual.' So the guy goes over to the poll parrot and said, 'Hello.' Parrot didn't say nothing. Fellow say, 'Polly wants a cracker?' Poll parrot didn't say nothing. Just kept on reading his newspaper just like he hadn't heard him. The fellow say again, 'Polly wants a cracker?' Finally, the poll parrot took his pipe out of his mouth, and lowered the newspaper and said, 'Nigger wants a watermelon?'"

Cathleen leaned her head out of the back of the house and sang out Elmo's name.

"EEElllllllMMMMooohhhhhh!"

"I got to go," Elmo said and ran off to the house. June Bug jumped down off the fence and followed him.

The next evening at the Smith's Anchorage Club, I asked Aunt Amanda if I could see Mrs. Smith's parrot.

"Not until after they've eaten. Now take these drinks out there."

"Then I can ask her?"

"Yeah, and don't be pestering that woman about no parrot!"

"Well, when can I see him?"

"Boy, take these drinks out there and don't spill them, and I'll tell her to let you see him! Now go on and do that."

The big fire roared in the fireplace as I placed the drinks on the table in front of Dr. Dawson. The extra drink was for the beautiful woman sitting with him.

"This is Mandy's boy," he said to her.

"This is Miss Lucy," he said, introducing me to the woman. "Miss Lucy is from the North."

"How are you?" she said.

"He's a marvelously gifted singer," Dr. Dawson said.

"Oh, is that right," Miss Lucy said. "Are you going to sing for us?"

"I don't know."

"Don't tease him," Dr. Dawson said.

When I turned back to the kitchen, Aunt Amanda was watching from the doorway, as usual.

"Now can I see the poll parrot?"

"Miss Smith wants you and Knee to sing for them."

"Can we see the poll parrot first?"

"I'll ask her. Come on." We went with her to the office, passing people who were dancing and drinking in the large dining room.

A young blond girl rushed up to Aunt Amanda.

"Amanda, I want you to meet my girlfriend!"

"Hello," Aunt Amanda said, smiling broadly.

"This is Linda. She goes to my school. And I've told her all about you." She turned to Linda. "Amanda is the best colored help in the world. She worked for my parents for years!"

"Yes, that's right," Aunt Amanda said. "I been knowing Billie since she was a little girl."

Then Billie turned to us.

"And these are the two little boys I told you about," Billie said. "Ain't they adorable. This is Morris and this is Cornelius."

"Say something nice to Billie," Aunt Amanda said. "You remember Billie?"

I couldn't remember her. Maybe I had seen her once or twice. I knew she was the daughter of the Smiths and that she had gone somewhere, "off to college," but I didn't know what that meant.

She leaned down to us. "Are you going to sing for us?"

"I want to see the poll parrot!" I told her.

"Mamma's old Polly?"

"Uh-huh!"

She grabbed me by the hand.

"Come, I'll take them to see Polly."

We went up some stairs and passed down a hall. In an empty office there was a cage with a big green bird in it.

"Well, here is Polly!"

I drew closer to the cage and looked at the bird. He had these large eyes that looked like doll's eyes and a nose that curved like the blade of a bowie knife.

"I'll let you and your brother play with him," she said and left us alone. As soon as the door closed, I leaned closer to Polly.

"Polly, say 'nigger'!" I told him. I waited but he didn't say anything, just looked at me. "Polly wants a cracker!" I said, expecting him to say, "Nigger wants a watermelon." But he said nothing.

"Say something, fool-ass bird," Knee demanded of him.

"If you don't say something, I'm gonna take you out and cut your hair off!"

Still nothing. We stuck our fingers in the cage and snatched them out before he had a chance to bite them. Still nothing.

"He scared because if he calls me a nigger I'm gonna kill him," I concluded.

"Me too," Knee said.

We played with the parrot until we heard Aunt Amanda calling us.

"Okay, we got to go now, Polly, but we gonna come back," we promised. "And you better say something. Okay?"

We opened the door to leave. Just as we were about to close it, the parrot said, "Nigger!"

We looked at each other, amazed and delighted with the insult.

We rushed to Aunt Amanda and whispered loudly with excitement.

"He called us a nigger!"

"You better leave that poll parrot alone," she said. "And come on here and sing."

That night we slowly planned how we were going to kill that poll parrot.

"Maybe we should wring his neck," I decided.

I shook my brother but he had fallen asleep. I couldn't sleep. Something was hanging over me. Like the feeling of dread whenever Aunt Amanda and Uncle Lofton talked to me about my father and mother. "Your father will be coming one day," Daddy would tell us, but we would deny it. No more would I play exhaustively with my brother, falling on the ground in our new suits and care not a whiff about the consequences. No more would I find mystery in a simple thing like a slingshot, or puzzle at the godlike power of a country doctor: my father was coming home.

PART TWO

~~~~~~

Dancing Without Shoes

Good morning, blues. Blues how
do you do?
Blues say, "I feel all right, but
I come to worry about you."
— TRADITIONAL

Chapter 14

Winter 1956, age 13

A slender black man in a gray suit stood across the room from me. He had a suitcase. He looked at me with a strange yet familiar smile.

"Do you know who that is?" Aunt Amanda asked me.

"Uh-huh!" I answered her.

"Go say hello to your father," she said.

I went up to Culphert.

"Hello," I said, and shook his hand. He smiled again.

"It's been a long time since we saw each other," he said. "You and your brother are almost grown up, aren't you?"

"I guess so."

"Come here!" He grabbed me and held me close to him. In a way I was really glad to see him too. I'm a part of him, I thought. He let me go, and I saw his smile. He had the same dark face, with high cheekbones and thick lips, as Aunt Amanda and Uncle Jack. He was me. I knew I had to get used to it.

He looked over at my brother.

"Come here, Knee," he said. Knee, always a bit shy, refused to go to him.

Uncle Lofton brought the suitcase into the house. "Well, I guess we can say welcome home," he said.

Amanda, who had disappeared briefly into the kitchen, now reappeared and said, "Everybody sit down and I'll fix us something."

119

Everybody ate as we usually did, but I felt uncomfortable. A new tension, a feeling of dread, made the tablecloth look funny to me, as if I'd never seen it before.

After dinner, while Culphert lay across the bed asleep, Knee and I went with Uncle Lofton to the barn to feed the pigs.

"Daddy, why did he come back?" Knee wanted to know. Were we going to be taken away? All those years of growing up with Uncle Lofton, we pretended he was our father. And yet, how could we blame Uncle Lofton, "Daddy"? He had told us repeatedly that he wasn't our real father, but we had refused to believe him. Now, we could no longer deny what he had told us all along.

"He wanted to see you boys," Uncle Lofton said. "He wants to be with his children."

"Uncle Lofton, where is he going to stay?" I asked him.

"He gonna stay here with us," he said, pouring the slop into the trough. "Where else can he stay? He ain't got nowhere else to stay. Elmo done moved out. He can't stay up there with your gramma. Too many people up there now."

As I watched the pigs eat the corn slop, I began to fear that our father's return was going to be disastrous. It was true that I had once longed for him to come, but that was when I was very little. Now I was not so sure.

What did his return mean to us? That our mother would return to us? That we would move to another place? I wouldn't see Willie and Kenneth anymore? Leon and his brother Willie wouldn't be our friends anymore? And our room. Who would stay in our room?

A few days later, Culphert took me and Knee in a pickup truck to Clarkton, where Aunt Greta, Flossie, Eli, Selina, and Linda lived. This was the first time we were alone together. We didn't want to go, but we had no choice.

I had already decided that I would show him how much we liked him. I was smart, so there would be plenty of times to impress him. Just as I could do with Uncle Lofton.

Culphert tried to be amusing, but he had little success with my brother and me. We didn't feel free with him. After he bought us ice cream on the ride up to Bladenboro, we decided that he was funny. He kept telling jokes and asking us questions. I did most of the answering.

"You want to see you mother?" he asked me.

"Uh-huh!" I said, to be polite.

"We going to go and see her together," he said, as he pulled into Rex Squire's place.

Every Monday was a big mule-trading special. When we arrived that day, we saw over a hundred horses and mules.

My brother and I were really excited as we pushed through all these cowboys, horse traders, mules, and horses.

"Now boys, this one here is slick as a ribbon," Rex Squire said to the crowd of men. "Somebody offered me a hundred dollars for her boys, but I like her too much for that. Oh, I wouldn't do that."

"I'll give you a hundred and ten, Rex?"

"Well, I wouldn't do that," Rex said. "This one here is slick as a ribbon, Josh. A fly could land on her and he'd slip off and break his neck. This one here is no stump sucker, boys. Get in there if you want to, boys. Now I've got a hundred and ten . . . a hundred and ten . . . boys. I got a good horse here, boys, if I never swap another horse in my life . . ."

The men were laughing and just enjoying the way the horse trader talked.

We walked around a bit, looking at horses and mules. I saw one man push another man.

"You goddamn Irish gypsies! The worst kind!"

"What he do!"

"He sold me a horse that had been goodnited!"

"He goodnite the horse?"

"Yeah!"

"What does that mean?" I asked Culphert.

"That's when they pull the testicles of the horse up and sew them high so that he looks young," he said.

I had heard a man shouting to another one, "Look at his cups!"

"What's cups?" I asked him.

He explained that the cups were the teeth. When they "mouth the cups," they look into the mouth to see how old the mule or horse is.

When we got back to the auction, Culphert started swapping with Rex for a mule.

"Cuffy, this mule is clean as a hat in a bandbox," Rex said to him, pointing to a short black mule. "I'll let you have him for fifty dollars. Harness and everything you need! You'll need a good turn plow, too."

While they were talking, I saw a tall mule nearby. He seemed

121

different from the others because of a bright, reddish, smooth hide.

"What about that one," I said to Culphert. "He looks big."

"Oh, you like that one?" he asked. He was delighted that I showed interest in buying the mule and started asking questions about the big red one.

"Him? That's no mule. A mule is fathered by a donkey. That one is fathered by a horse. That's a henny!"

"What do you want for him?"

"It's a she. I donno. Give twenty-five."

"Okay, I'll take her."

We loaded the big red mule on the back of the pickup truck and brought her to my grandfather's farm. The farm was five miles from the nearest neighbor. It stood in the clearing of a forest of tall, long-leaf pine trees. The farm was so far away from Bolton that everybody referred to it as "the swamp."

At home, I was excited about buying the mule and told Uncle Lofton about it. But I had no idea why Culphert bought the mule.

"Why did he buy a red mule, Daddy?"

"Didn't you want him to buy him?"

"I didn't care," I said. "What is he going to do with him?"

"He's gonna plow him, what you think. Now, Morris, you got better sense than that! You know what mules are for."

"Who's going to plow him?"

Daddy looked at me and laughed. Did he mean I would plow the big red mule? Plowing was not a bad thing, and I didn't mind the big red mule. Maybe I would like to learn to plow. But maybe Culphert would plow the mule himself.

The next day, Culphert took us to the farm and hitched the mule up to a plow. We thought that he was going to plow himself.

"Here," he said to me. "Get behind that plow!"

I placed myself behind the plow, grabbing both handles. He took the plow lines and threaded them through the reins on the harness and handed them to me.

"Now get the mule moving," he instructed me.

I knew a little bit about plowing from seeing it. So I knew how to tell the mule to move.

"Git up!" I shouted, and Big Red began to move off down the row.

"Stop her!" Culphert shouted.

"Whoa!" I shouted. Big Red stopped. She was a well-trained mule.

"Tell her 'Gee' and 'Haw,' " he said, and I gave the commands, which were right and left respectively.

"Now plow all the way down and back," Culphert said, "and let me see how you do."

I plowed the furrow all the way down to the end of the row. When I came to the end of the row, I was supposed to swing the plow around by leaning back on it so that the mule could lift up its weight, but I was too small to lift it up. Big Red helped me out by leaning over so that the plow popped out of the ground. I pushed down on the handles so that the heel of the plow rode the ground and slid around and headed back.

After I had plowed a few rows, my brother tried it. After we finished the field, Culphert showed us how to feed the mule with hay from the barn. He showed us the place for the harness and where to store the plow.

"Uncle Lofton," I said that evening as Daddy and I were coming back to the house, "I plowed today!"

"You did?" he said proudly. "Now you're a plowboy!"

"I'm going to help Culphert farm," I said, "but every night I will come back here to stay with you!"

Uncle Lofton didn't say anything.

"Uncle Lofton, we don't have to go stay with Culphert, do we?"

"Now listen, you boys know that you are not my children. But I have raised you like mine. But that's your real daddy. If he wants to take you with him, it's his right."

I was too angry and hurt to speak.

A few days later, my mother and me and my brother and Culphert moved into the house. Our mother had been living right in the town all this time, I realized as we drove into the swamp. What had she been doing? Why didn't she come see us?

We didn't call her mother, because we were nearly strangers to each other. We called her "Dorothy."

After driving five miles into the swamp, we drove a mile down a dirt road, at the end of which sat the house in a clearing. This shack that sat on four cinder blocks like a fat hen was our new home. We got out with our clothes in a suitcase and entered the house.

Over the next few days, I began to compare this new house

with what I had been used to. There was no electricity or running water. For lights we had kerosene lamps. For water, there was a pump outside the back door. Farther, back toward the creek, was an outhouse. Between the outhouse and the house was a chicken coop, a smokehouse, and a potato bank.

The house was the one Uncle Lofton and Aunt Amanda had lived in when they got married in 1939. Grand Papa Cecil had built it himself, from the timber he got from the clearing.

It had four rooms, and a big, red brick chimney that was opened on both sides. On one side of the chimney was the kitchen and on the other side was the living room. In the first weeks, Culphert was busy covering it with gray shingles. He put Sheetrock in their room, but me and my brother's room was covered with newspaper to keep the wind from coming in the cracks.

While Culphert put up fresh Sheetrock and wallpaper, Dorothy washed the floors. Sugarboy and Lindsey—Dorothy's brothers— came and cut wood for the fireplace.

We soon learned that there was little time for the childhood pastimes we had enjoyed with Uncle Lofton. We had to come home from school, take off our school clothes, and hitch up Big Red and plow. Just before nightfall, we had to unhitch the mule, feed her, feed the pigs, shell corn for the chickens, cut wood and bring it in. After we ate we had to wash the dishes and clean the lampshades. In the morning we had to make the fire before Culphert got up so the house would be warm for him.

We didn't have many visitors except Aunt Amanda and Uncle Lofton occasionally, and once or twice Grand Papa Cecil would come down on his buggy and mule.

I got to know my mother again—or perhaps for the first time. She would tell us stories about her father, Sam Waddell, whom we never knew. She told us about how he worked at the Big Mill in Bolton, and how as a girl she had to take him his dinner of fatback, Irish potatoes, and corn bread with green onions.

"Why didn't you want us when Culphert was gone?" I asked her, one day when I had managed to get up the courage.

"I wanted you, but Manda kept after me, kept worrin me to take you boys."

"But couldn't you take care of us?"

"Not as good as Lofton could. Lofton had a job. Nobody else had a job. My brothers were too small to work."

She told us that after her father's death, the only person old enough to work was her older brothers Tootsie and J. B., neither of whom had a regular job. They worked on the farm for white people. They had a cow. "We lived off milk and butter and corn bread," she said. She told us she couldn't take care of us, and thought that Uncle Lofton and Aunt Amanda could do a better job because they had more money.

Our most consistent visitor was not a member of our family but a white man, Elwood Martin. Elwood Martin was a good friend of my grandfather's. He owned the land adjoining Papa's.

Elwood Martin would come down almost every other day. He'd stop his truck and talk with us for hours. It didn't matter who he talked to. If Culphert wasn't there, he would talk to Dorothy. If Dorothy wasn't there, he would stop by the field where I would be working and talk to me about how much he respected Grand Papa Cecil.

All the Browns respected Elwood. "All of Cecil's children think a lot of me," he would say, "cause I think a lot them."

Sugarboy and Lindsey liked him, too. Lindsey and Sugarboy had a unique joking relationship with Elwood. The most particular thing about Elwood Martin was his long nose, and both Lindsey and Sugarboy called him Snout, to his face, and Elwood would only laugh. They talked about coon hunting and deer hunting as if nothing else existed in the world.

But most of my days were spent alone, working the fields behind Big Red. One day, however, when I was plowing, I saw Culphert's truck pulling up. When it got nearer, I saw that he had Billy Pyatt with him. Billy Pyatt was related to the Geechies, who lived in the Quarter, the section of Bolton where only blacks lived. Billy Pyatt walked behind him, carrying a new straw hat. A few years older than me, quiet spoken, and very dark, Billy Pyatt was a boy who went his own way.

"This boy's gonna help you," Culphert said. "Tie the mule up and come help us."

We got in the truck and went to the barn and loaded five hundred-pound bags of fertilizer on the truck and brought them to the field.

When we got back out in the field, the sun was blazing hot, even though it was only about nine o'clock. I could always tell the time by the shadows on the dirt.

125

As Billy Pyatt began to pour the fertilizer into the buckets, I thought of the time I had seen him dancing in JC's. Billy Pyatt was doubtless the best dancer I'd ever seen. A quiet, reticent person in conversation, on the dance floor he was a madman. He had this one dance called the Buzzard Lope that was a knockout to watch. He would flap his elbows like a buzzard flaps his wings to fly.

When we came to the end of a row, I said to him, "Billy Pyatt, let me see you do the Buzzard Lope!"

"Naw, I ain't got time to be foolin with you, Morris. Culphert got me out here paying me to work! Ain't no time to be dancin!"

Just then one of the buzzards swamped down over the top of the pines.

"What's that?"

"Brother Buzzard's comin to eat his supper!" I told him. He stood up and watched the buzzards circling. When they landed, they flipped their wings. Billy started imitating the way they walked by sticking his elbows out and flapping them.

"Oh, man, that's tough!" I said, to encourage him. He responded by sticking out his neck like the buzzards did.

When he saw how much I wanted to see him dance, he said he'd make a deal with me. If I didn't tell Culphert, he'd show me. He showed me his version of the Ranky Tank, in which he put his weight on his front foot and pushed himself across the field with his back foot. Then he did something called the Shake Hips, and showed me how to make a turn on the toes without toppling over.

"Let me do it!" I exclaimed. I tried it but my toes dug in the dirt and I could go only halfway around before falling down.

"You need shoes to dance in," Billy Pyatt said. Suddenly, for the first time ever in my life, I desired a pair of shoes. Usually, when I had to go back to school the feel of shoes in September hurt my feet, didn't feel natural. Now, I thought, if I had shoes, I could move like Billy Pyatt.

"But can't you show me a little bit more?" I said.

"I know what I'll do," he said, and picked up a piece of wood and laid it down flat. "Now dance on this."

He demonstrated his technique, and I'd get up on the board and practice it.

We danced and danced until noontime when we heard the rumbling of my father's truck coming. In the distance, I could see the dust rising. Panic went through me.

126

"Now, what you gonna do!" Billy Pyatt exclaimed. "What Culphert gonna say when he see we still got his fertilizer and ain't put it in the field?"

I had an idea. I grabbed a bag of the fertilizer and carried it to the ditch which separated the fields and threw it in. But I had to tear the bags off it so that this could be shown as evidence that it had been emptied. Jumping into the ditch, I ripped the bag open and pulled out the paper sack and dropped it along the end of the row.

The truck rolled up, stopped, and Culphert got out with a bag.

"How many bags you finished?" he asked, looking at the empty sacks. "Oh, I see you done gone through those bags already. That's good, boys."

"Thank you," Billy Pyatt said, his hand reaching out for the brown paper sack. Opening it, he found a poor boy sandwich and a Pepsi. Culphert gave me a similar bag.

"I'm gonna be back in about three hours, and you should have this field finished by then," he said, and got into the truck and left.

"Morris, you are one slick coon," Billy Pyatt laughed after Culphert had gone. I was proud of the way I had tricked Culphert, and felt justified in my trickery, since he was, in my estimation, a trickster, who had stolen my brothers and me from our home with Uncle Lofton and Aunt Amanda. I felt I had done something good.

With his new respect for my cleverness, Billy Pyatt showed me all the dance steps he knew. Whenever he came to work for us, all he had to do was teach me dancing and I would do all the work.

"Dorothy," I said that night at home, "I want some shoes."

"For what?"

"I want to go in to JC's shop," I said. JC's was the local Bolton juke joint. It was the place everybody went to listen to blues music and fight and drink and gamble and dance and love.

"What you goin to do in JC's?" she wanted to know.

"I been there before!"

"When did you go in JC Himes' Place?" In the way Dorothy was smiling, I knew that she had been there too, or at the very least, she knew about it.

"Uncle Lofton used to let me and Knee go when we went to Billy Lewis's and Mr. Holmes to buy stuff." Billy Lewis was the white man's store we had to shop at for farm supplies. His store was one of the last ones on the block before you got to the nigger stores. Between Billy Lewis's place and JC's there was only a small strip of no-man's-land, about twenty yards of ground, and a ditch.

"What that man let you younguns in there for?"

"To look at the people dancing!"

"Dancing? What you know about dancing?"

"A lot," I said, smiling subtly. I always had the feeling that I wanted to tell her something but I couldn't in words; I wanted to signal something to her, without taking the responsibility for the message. So I resorted to secret expressions and gestures.

"Can you dance?" she asked.

"Yeah," I said. "Wanna see?"

"Show me, then."

I backed up to the corner of the kitchen and then started across just as I had seen Billy Pyatt do and then when I got to the middle, I wailed like mad, ending up on the table.

"That boy can dance!" Dorothy said, as if she was talking to a large crowd of people. "Where did you learn to dance like that?"

"I just learned it," I said, not trusting her enough to tell her about the dancing lessons Billy Pyatt had been giving us.

"Well, we better get you some shoes," she said, "cause you sho can dance!"

We laughed and danced around and I discovered that she was easy to like, had a sense of humor, and that she really did love us.

When Culphert came home that night, Dorothy said to him at the supper table, "Morris wants some shoes."

"For what? You can't plow a mule in shoes," he demanded.

"He wants to go out!"

"Out where!" he shouted, almost going into a rage. "What the hell you talking about! Dancing! If I catch you even thinking about dancing, nigger, I'll break your neck! You keep your ass down on that field. Stay your ass behind the plow!"

My mother said, "It's only natural. He wants to go out sometimes, just like you did."

"If I'd stayed behind the plow like my daddy tried to tell me, I'd never have gotten in that trouble."

"But you can't blame me for your life," I wanted to say, but I knew that if I didn't want a beating, I'd better not say it.

"Dancing is all you *black niggers* think about!" he went on. "Dancing and whoring and drinking and gambling. When do we ever own anything! If I catch you in JC, *you'll never forget it.* Do you understand that, boy?"

He was staring straight at me.

"Yes, suh!"

My father, it seemed to me, could do anything he wanted and nobody would blame him. *Nobody blamed him! Nobody could stop him!* He could take us from Uncle Lofton and treat us any way he wanted.

That evening as the sun was setting, I came up the road with Big Red and I saw the Buick coming down the road. It was Uncle Lofton and Aunt Amanda! Rushing to the stable, I unhooked Big Red by the time they had driven in the driveway. I dashed up to Daddy and threw my arms around him.

"How you boys doin?" Daddy asked me.

"I don't like it down here," I said to him, afraid to look at Culphert, who stood in the doorway.

"Now, you boys come with me," Uncle Lofton said, sensing trouble. He walked down the road with us.

"See, now you see why Culphert bought Big Red, don't you?" Daddy said, when we were out of earshot of Culphert. "I told you one day your real daddy would come back and now he's back!"

"Yeah, but Daddy, he don't have to be so *mean!*"

"What's wrong, Morris?" Uncle Lofton asked me when he saw that I was really upset.

"Daddy, he works me too hard!"

"Well, you gettin to be big boys now," he said. "You spoze to work."

"Daddy, he beats me!"

Uncle Lofton listened to us as we lodged our complaints against Culphert. Did he know what Culphert was really like?

"No, listen, you boys got to listen to me. If we go strictly by the law, you're his children. But if you go by the heart, you mine. Now, you got to stay with Culphert and Dorothy, that's your parents. But I want you to try to understand them, too. Try to not take them too serious. Morris, do you understand?"

I thought about the plowing.

"But Daddy, did you have to plow when you was my age?"

"Oh, yes I had to do it, much younger than you!"

"How old, Daddy?"

"Oh, eleven."

"Daddy, I ain't but thirteen!"

"You have to do what your father tells you to, but now listen to me, and I don't want you to tell anybody about this, but if it gets too rough, y'all know where I live. Do you understand, you can always come home to me, and nobody'll bother you."

We walked back to the house, and Culphert came out to meet us. I could tell there was going to be a fight.

We were standing in front of our house between two large oak trees which had a bench between them. When the trees were saps, my grandfather had placed a board between them; now, twenty-five years later, the wooden plank had become a part of the trees.

"Culphert, you got to let me take these boys out for some culture," Uncle Lofton said.

"They go to work, Lofton."

"When I had em I'd drive places and they could have some fun looking out the window, reading the billboards."

"Well, they can't do that now."

"Let me take them off to Whiteville with me when I go tomorrow."

"Alright, but don't keep them too long."

The next day, Aunt Amanda had the perfect solution to my problem.

"If he want some dancing shoes," she said, on the way to Whiteville, "let him plant his own bacco on his own land, and make his own money."

"But I don't have no land, Aunt Manda?"

"We'll see about that," she said. "Grandpa will let you have a piece of his land down there in on the place. I'll talk to him about it."

"I can have my own land to plant tobacco on?" I asked. The idea of having my own land was a dream come true. I didn't like working for Culphert, but the thought that I could have all the money I made from my own land excited me.

"Will you ask Grandpa for us?" Knee asked.

"Alright," Uncle Lofton said. "That's what you boys gonna do. Grow your own tobacco, and have your own money to buy anything you want to."

"Okay!"

The next day, we saw Grand Papa Cecil coming down the road on his wagon. As his wagon rolled closer, I recognized his familiar hat, an old elegant black Stetson, and his dog.

"Boys, I'm gonna give you a piece of land," he said, getting off his wagon.

Grandpa moved with great authority across the field and we followed him. Like my father, he had a great presence, but unlike my father, his life was no mystery to me. I could say what I wanted around him, and ask him anything, and he would respond, first with a laugh, and then with wisdom.

Grandpa took us across the field and through a small footpath. I knew where we were going. We were going to a small opening in the green pines to a piece of land we called "Papa's Place." It was the first piece of land that he bought from the horse dealer, Rex Squire.

Papa stopped and pointed to the stretch of field that suddenly appeared before us.

"Now you boys see this here land?"

"Yes, sir."

It was about a quarter of a mile and was surrounded on both sides with a wall of young pine trees. A cover of green weeds grew over it. Through the trees the sun shone through to it. In another hour, it would be bathed in sunshine. And at night, the moon seemed to hang over it as if the moon had no place else to go. I knew all about "Papa's Place" because it always made me feel special when I went there.

"Our property runs over to that fence, you see here," he said, "and that piece of land you see here is ours. Now, you and your brother say you want shoes. Well, if you want shoes so bad, then you have to work for them. If you and your brother want to do that, then you can have this field to grow your own tobacco on it and corn, whatever you want, and with the money for that you can buy your school clothes."

He turned to me.

"You boys know how to farm?"

"Yes, Grand Papa. We can do it."

Since we were little, we had watched Uncle Lofton farm, and he was a good farmer. He worked on the railroad, but his side job, as he called it, his "side line," was farming.

"Well, I'm let you boys have this to grow yo crops on."

I was so proud; it was as if he were a great king and had bestowed a great responsibility on my shoulder. I loved him, and because of that land, I loved him even more now that I was going to farm it.

At the dinner table that evening, I tried to explain the setup to Culphert.

"We want to grow tobacco," I said.

"Alright," Culphert said. "But you have to do it when you're not working for me. Do it when you've finished doing what I told you to do."

"Okay," I agreed. I would get Daddy to help us, I thought, and it would be the greatest field of tobacco ever grown.

"I may look like I'm hard on you," he said, "but I ain't. I'm just trying to show you how hard it is because you are black people. The white people don't give us nothing. All this land you see here, your granddaddy, my daddy, bought himself. He worked for a dollar a day to get seven hundred dollars to buy this land."

We wanted to show Culphert that we could make our own money.

My brother and I worked that piece of land as if it were our own. After we had finished working on Culphert's fields, we would rush to our field and do all the things that we had seen Uncle Lofton do. I dreamed of new shoes and clothes which I would wear and which would dazzle everybody when I walked into JC's shop and danced.

After school and on the weekends, I had to plow in Culphert's field. We had five or six fields on that farm, and at the end of each field I had discovered a perfect shade tree to rest Big Red and read. Culphert forbade me to work Big Red in the hot sun. If something happened to Big Red, something terrible would happen to me. Big Red was a big investment, and I had to be careful with her.

One day I was sitting under my favorite tree at the end of a row reading when I saw Culphert coming up the field. I didn't dislike him; in fact, I was happy to see him, because I had finally decided that I would ask him about his prison life. Uncle Lofton said I should "talk to your real daddy about that." Now I would. But as he approached I saw that he had a plow line in his hand.

132

"What you doin?" he asked me, threateningly.

"Oh, just reading a book," I said. I turned the book over so that he could see the title. This caused him great alarm.

"*Little Women!*" he said, smoldering, as if he knew the book and had read it himself. His fist was tightening on the rope. Was he going to hit me? Why would he hit me? What had I done? Did he object to my reading about little white girls?

"The war is over, Mr. March is safely at home, busy with his books . . . ?" I said to him, reading a quote from the book.

"Yeah," he said, glaring again as he tightened the rope around his fist. "The war sure is over!"

I felt uncomfortable and backed away as I watched him reach out for me. "I'm goin to teach you to read a damn book when you should be working."

"But it's just a book about Mr. March coming home from the war?"

"Yeah, Mr. March, is it? I'm going to Mr. March you. Boy, you know Mr. March is gonna get you an ass whipping! Are you a sissy, boy?" he asked me. He grabbed my shirt collar with his left hand, snatched me up off the ground, and dangled me in the air. *Little Women* went flying into the wet, black furrow.

As he sat me back down to the ground, he lifted the plow line in his right hand; I waited for the lick to fall.

"What the hell you doin reading in a goddamn book when you should be workin! If I ever catch you with a book in your hand when you suppose to be plowing this damn mule, I'm gonna whip yo ass till the cows come home. Do you understand me?"

"Yes, sir!"

He let me down and I skulked away. I cried at the dinner table that night, and Dorothy got quiet.

"Damn books!" he screamed from the supper table, frowning at me. All of his bitterness and disappointment in life seemed to have found expression in this crime. I felt afraid and wished I was back with Uncle Lofton.

"This boy ain't no good, woman!" he howled into her face. "Lofton durn ruint him!" Dorothy was silent, afraid of being hit at any moment.

I looked at her across the checked tablecloth, at the yellow candlelight flickering across her rigid face. She was scared to death of him. While Culphert ate, she held her breath; only the sound of his eating and breathing filled the room. As I listened to his sounds, I realized how completely Uncle Lofton and Aunt Amanda had fooled us. Here we were, imprisoned by that escaped criminal! How could I get away?

"You ought not get mad with Lofton and Amanda, after all they have done for you, and for these children. Now, you know that ain't right," Dorothy said, when his rage had subsided.

"What you keep bringin Lofton in this? You think he's such a great man? You take the side of these people against me! You don't think I know how to raise my own children?" he said, his voice heavy with threat again.

When it was safe, I eased away from the table back to my room. Later, I heard noises coming from their room. She sounded like he was hurting her, and I felt rage again. Then she sounded like she was trying to catch her breath and he was strangling her. And then she laughed and sounded happy. I didn't understand it. When I lay awake at Uncle Lofton's and Aunt Amanda's, I never heard them make a sound. I fell asleep.

As the summer passed, Elwood Martin noticed how puny Culphert's crop was compared to the patch that me and my brother planted on "Papa's Place." Field hands begin to make the same comment, and one day, when he was talking to Elwood Martin about it, Culphert said, "I can't figure out why the weeds in the ditch are growing so much!" I looked over to the ditch and saw that the place where I had thrown the fertilizer was now high with tall bushes.

The fertilizer had caused the wild bushes and dog fenders to shoot up to the sky. I grew fearful that my evil deed would be discovered. If I had made a mistake with Uncle Lofton, I could tell him that I had made a mistake. But with Culphert I was afraid to even open my mouth.

"Looks like some fertilizer hit them weeds," Elwood Martin observed from his truck.

"I can't figure it out," Culphert said. "And the corn looks like it's gonna die!"

"Did you put any fertilizer in the corn, Culphert?" Elwood said, laughing.

"Yeah, I put fertilizer on that corn," Culphert said.

"If you put fertilizer on it," Elwood said, "the corn should be growing, Culphert, and not the weeds."

When Elwood was gone, I saw Culphert go over to the ditch and reach down and pull up a piece of that fertilizer sack.

"Boy, you didn't put that fertilizer in the ground, did you?" he said, looking at me and holding the paper sack up for me to see.

"Yes, suh, I did."

"You didn't!"

"Yes I did!"

He came closer to me and I ran. He ran after me, screaming, "Nigger, you lying to me!" He grabbed a switch from the branch that had grown so strong.

"Now, I'm gonna take one of these switches from this ditch and whip your ass with it."

I had to stand there while he peeled the switch.

"Turn around," he demanded. I stood there and closed my eyes while he beat me, whipping me across my back with the switches, but I wouldn't cry.

He grabbed me by the collar and dragged my face up to his. "You think that you're grown, don't you?"

I refused to answer him, out of spite.

"Don't you?" he shouted, bringing the switch down on my behind. "Think you a man, don't you! Answer me!"

"No!"

"You answer me, 'Yes sir!' "

He hit me again. The pain was too much for me and I yielded. The pain shot through my body and I cried.

"Don't you *Ever! Ever! Ever! Ever! Don't you Ever-Let-Me-See-You-Reading-A-Book—Again—*"

I tried to get away from him, but he grabbed me by my neck and put it under his arm in a vise, and whaled me with the switch until he was tired; he rested, still panting for breath.

"Now get that damn mule and get back in that field!" I picked up my straw hat and untied Big Red.

I hated Culphert from that moment on. I cried and moped until Uncle Lofton and Aunt Amanda showed up to see us.

"Culphert, I'm tell you this to you face," he said. "By law, they yours. But by heart, they mine."

Culphert replied, "You ruin the oldest boy, Lofton. All he wants to do is *read*."

"Now, Culphert, you know yourself that reading is good for these children."

"How the hell I'm gonna get this crop in, man, if these boys don't know how to work."

"You could do some of it yourself," Uncle Lofton said. This made Culphert hot.

At this point, Aunt Amanda took over.

"If y'all don't want them, let us have em back," she said.

"We want them," Dorothy said, leaning out the window.

"Well, if you want them, treat em like something," Daddy said. This made me nervous. Up to this time, I had clung to the hope, admittedly improbable, that we would be allowed to return to Uncle Lofton and Aunt Amanda.

"Lofton, I think I know what's good for my own children," Culphert said. "Me and Dorothy getting along just fine with our children."

There was nothing more to be said.

"Well, you got to send them to school. They never missed a day when they was with me," Uncle Lofton said, defeated.

"They got to *work*," Culphert said. "Not *read*."

"And another thing is this. We never laid a hand on these boys," he said. "They wasn't shy and scared when we had em." That was to let Culphert know that he knew he had beat me. That made me feel a little bit better.

As the darkness descended, I stood watching Uncle Lofton and Aunt Amanda roll away from me in the Buick like a memory already fading.

"Daddy!" I could not resist the impulse to hug them one more time and ran to the car. Knee was right beside me.

"We don't want to stay here!" Knee cried out.

"No, Daddy, please!"

We screamed and cried. Daddy had to stop the car and talk to us again. We cried and cried, begging to be allowed to spend just another night back at home. Daddy said he would come see us the very next day. This cooled us out, the fact that he had said it so that Culphert heard him. They went home, and we had to retrace our steps back to Culphert.

When I turned to face Culphert, I lowered my head and rushed to get out of his presence. I had shown him that I distrusted him, and now I feared he would punish me for it.

That night he was angry with my mother.

"The crops are ruined! He didn't put the fertilizer in the ground! He put it in a ditch! If we were selling bushes, we would be rich, but we ain't! I'm gonna kill that boy! What kind of idiot did Lofton raise!"

The hot boiling yellow sun faded with the passing days, and the unbearable July and August heat was over. Now cool breezes were more frequent. It was time then to harvest the tobacco and take it to the market, to the "pack house."

Mine and Knee's crop grew to golden harvest, and when we sold it on the market we got the highest price for it. But Culphert's was a complete failure, and he assumed that the money from our acre was his also. He needed the money, he said, because another baby was coming.

"He took our money," we said to Uncle Lofton who came to take us to Whiteville to get shoes and clothes for school.

"It's rough on Culphert," Daddy said.

"But he took our money," Knee said.

"I know it hurt you boys," Daddy said. "He shouldn't done that."

I couldn't stop crying. I wanted to like Culphert, but I also wanted to enjoy the independence and fairness Uncle Lofton had allowed me. I felt cheated by Culphert, robbed of the labor I had put into the land. Uncle Lofton would never do that, and that was what made it so painful. He was always encouraging me and my brother by rewarding us for our industriousness. If Uncle Lofton promised me he would give me something if I succeeded in a challenging endeavor, he had always kept his word.

"He told us we could have the money we made on the land. And we worked that field every day. We grew a lot of bacco."

"I know, boys, but it's hard on Cuffy," Uncle Lofton said.

"But why do we have to stay with him!" Knee cried.

"He's yo daddy," Uncle Lofton said.

"But he cheated us!" I wept. "He took all our school money!"

"And we worked for it!"

"I know you boys did," Uncle Lofton said. "I know it. But the fact is, you boys got to understand something. Culphert ain't no farmer. If he had been a good farmer, his crops would have yield. He doesn't know as much about farming as you two boys do."

This was further proof that Uncle Lofton had, indeed, taught us something. Culphert always said that we were lazy, idle boys who were just as contented to read a book as plow a furrow.

"You see he didn't know what he was doin," Uncle Lofton said. "If he did, he wouldn't have to jump on that little bit of money you and Knee made. He too shamed to admit he don't know that much about farming."

"But he always talkin bout he know about everything," Knee said, "and he don't know nothin. I hate him!"

"Daddy, what did Culphert do that they put him in prison?" I asked.

"Now, you have to ask him that. He should tell you that. Then you will be able to grow up."

Chapter 15

~~~~~~

One day in school a boy called me and my brother "swamp rabbits." Other boys joined him in ridiculing us. I was so ashamed of where we lived that I could barely lift my head to shout back at them.

When I lived in town with Uncle Lofton, I was very popular at the school, but we had fallen so low in status that everybody could pick at us. My little love affairs with girls like Violet May were now out of the question because nobody would ever think of going with a swamp rabbit. The idea would bring laughter to any of the kids in the fourth grade or above.

But everything changed when one day a magician came to our school; I volunteered to go up on the stage and assist him with his tricks.

Although I tried to discover his secrets, my greatest thrill was taking part of the credit for the success of the magic. The magician had convinced me that I shared some of his power. After I left the stage, I wanted to learn how to do tricks. I enjoyed the way it felt to have people ask me how the magician did his tricks.

I recalled how Dr. Dawson used books to become a doctor. I knew I could become a magician if I had the books, so I sent away a coupon I found in the back of a comic book for my first magic kit and started doing magic tricks.

Soon, I could make a silk handkerchief disappear, or change its color from blue to yellow. I could make coins appear out of my nose and disappear in my ear. I knew card tricks and went around with a deck demonstrating my magical skills.

After a few months, I decided that I was going to be a plowboy forever unless I became a magician. I had hidden my magic kit in a tree so that when I was alone with Big Red I'd go to it, lift off a piece of rotten wood, brush away a thin layer of dirt, and pull out the kit. I practiced my sleight of hand in a mirror I propped up. Sometimes I would read about a trick, and then I would plow awhile, turning what I had read over and over in my head.

In my deep concentration, I began to notice things which had escaped me before: the coolness of the freshly turned dirt as my bare feet eased down into the farrow, the choir of birds that sat invisibly in the pine saps that crowded the end of the field, and the act of plowing itself.

In spite of the monotony, I was still captivated by the techniques of plowing. You had to put pressure on the plow handles which would turn the plow point up; this movement controlled how deep you went into the ground. If you let the handle ease up, not applying too much pressure, the plow point would go deep into the soil. This was called "breaking ground" but had to be done by men with big muscles.

The kind of plowing I was doing was throwing furrows on the edge of the corn. The plow handles had to be held down so that the tip skimmed the surface about two inches, and when you did it right, the point of the plow would skirt under the dirt and send a wave of soil up and off from the plow wing, like the prow of a ship plowing through water, and this wave of dirt, an arc of wet dirt in motion, would sail though the air and wrap itself protectively around the corn stalk.

The fresh coat of dirt not only protected the young corn from the weather and insects but also nurtured it. Sometimes fertilizer had been dropped by the corn so that the wetness of the fresh layer of dirt would dissolve it.

I felt that I was doing something that had a purpose to it, and this made me feel useful. When I came to the end of a row, I would turn and look at it. Pride and accomplishment swept over me.

Big Red helped in that she was an exceptionally intelligent mule. She only had to be told once to "gee" and she would move right. She was tall, so that her strides were long and smooth. She also had extremely good hearing. When she heard Culphert's truck two miles off, she would shake her ears and look over at me and snort her nose. This was her signal that Culphert was coming. It gave me enough time to close and hide all my books and equipment in the woods before his truck rolled up to the end of the field.

Then I would be subject to Culphert's inspections. He would get out and come over and look at the field like a prison warden inspecting a chain gang.

If he didn't like what I did, if the dirt was too high on the corn, he would break out into a rage. Sometimes the young corn would be too weak to withstand the heavy thrust of dirt and would break under the deluge, like a tree demolished by a gigantic mud slide. If I didn't dig them out before Culphert saw them, my life would have been in danger when he arrived.

Occasionally, the inevitable would happen: a root or stump left in the field would hit the plow point, and it would break. Culphert imagined that I did it on purpose, or that I was not paying attention. Then he would get mad at me because he would have to drive to Bolton and get another one, which meant that he would have to pay for it.

When I worked in the fields next to the house, I could always smell my mother cooking lunch and she would yell to me to tie Big Red and come eat. But when we worked fields that were down the road apiece, and I couldn't smell the scent of the food, Knee would run part of the way, stop, and yell for me to come eat.

For lunch my mother often cooked a squirrel which had been killed that day either by Lindsey or somebody else on my mother's side of the family. Rarely did Culphert kill anything for us to eat.

Sometimes it wasn't squirrel, but venison, or as we sometimes called it, deer. Dorothy learned to cook it from her mother, and she had learned it from her mother, who had been raised in the big kitchen of the Oakland Plantation. Dorothy would stew the deer with potatoes and onions she got from her "patch." She served it to us with corn bread and lemonade.

At these times, during lunch, when we were alone, I would ask her questions, to find out why Culphert beat me.

"He don't mean it," she would say. But I had the whelps on my behind to prove that he did mean it.

"Why do he work us so hard?" I asked her.

"Lord, he doin the best he can!"

"We want to go back and stay with Uncle Lofton," Knee said, his elbows on the table, his head between his fists.

141

Dorothy looked at him.

"Boy, don'cha let that man hear you say that!" She'd lean back. "Don't get me beat up!"

I would feel depressed and sad for her, but I was not able to express it and remained silent.

For the rest of the afternoon, I'd plow meditatively. All sorts of notions, jokes, fragments of memories would float through my head, but the ones that wouldn't go away had to do with how my brother and I would escape from Culphert.

During this miserable time, my mother had a baby, a boy. His name was Donald Ray Brown, and because he had such a round head at birth we nicknamed him "Ping Pong." A year after that, the first girl in our family, Dorothy Elaine Brown, and we called her Elaine.

We were also blessed with Uncle Lindsey's visits. He would come to cut wood, or capture the wild honey in the trees or hunt. He had always told us that he would come to get us in the middle of the night to go hunting, and that we had to be prepared. And though every night we went to sleep talking about Lindsey coming, every morning we would awaken to discover that he had not come.

And then one night, it happened. I felt somebody pulling my foot. I woke up, thinking that it was my brother. But then I saw his curly black hair reflected in the moonlight that shone through the window.

"Wake up, man!" And I recognized Lindsey's voice. "Wake up, if you want to go hunting."

It was Lindsey, alright!

"Knee!" I shook him and then felt down beneath him to see if he had pissed in the bed. He hadn't. "Git up!" I whispered in his ear. "Lindsey is here!" The information went to his brain with emergency stamped on it, and his head popped up. "We goin hunting?"

"Yeah!"

We eased out of bed and out of the house without waking my parents up. The moon was full and I noticed our shadows against the chicken coop as we went down the path to the back woods. Lindsey told us to put our hands in each other's back pocket and not to speak a word.

We walked through the dark woods and felt the tall, silent pine trees watching us. A coon dog cried on the other side of the creek, and an ominous, sudden shrill of an owl startled me. During the day I had often crossed the creek and walked in this part of the woods, but at night I was lost.

Lindsey stopped and waited and watched. Finally, he spotted the prey. I watched his face and his eyes to see what he saw. He was looking at a dark form in the corner of the field.

As we watched, the shape changed under the shifting light of the moon that was sailing through the clouds. Right before our eyes this dark glob transformed itself into a beautiful brown creature with startling eyes. With deft motions, Lindsey slipped the rifle up, switched on the flashlight, and fired a shot right between the buck's eyes. It dropped and thrashed its feet.

Another one stood there dazed, not knowing what had happened. Lindsey cocked the shotgun again, holding the light steady at the same time, and shot him as he turned to run.

He handed me the flashlight and ran over to cut their throats. I stood there, shaking with fear and excitement. Knee was scared too, and I felt his grip on my arm as we waited while Lindsey pulled one of them into the bushes and threw the other one on his shoulders and started back up the path. I was beaming with excitement, barely able to wait until I could tell my mother what had happened.

When I got out of bed the next morning, I went to the kitchen. The house felt emptied of Culphert. I looked in their room and saw only my mother getting up. I went back through the kitchen and opened the back door.

Lindsey had the deer hung by his legs like a hog. He had cut the guts from the carcass. I saw the deer antlers mounted on the smokehouse door and ran down to inspect them closer.

"Hey, Morris," Lindsey said.

"What happened to the other deer?" I asked him.

"I couldn't find him," he said. "He will probably go off somewhere and die. Look in the sky in a few days and you'll see Knee Buzzard up there lookin for him."

Dorothy cooked the deer for lunch, and Lindsey sat with us under the tree in the front yard and drank some lemonade and told us stories about buzzard. It was early spring and the dogwoods were blooming.

When he had to leave, we were sad. With his gun slung on his shoulder, and some of the deer meat Dorothy had wrapped in a newspaper under his arm, he walked out the door and was gone.

We ran from the table to catch him as he reappeared, rounding the tobacco field, heading for the road. We watched with sad eyes until he disappeared down the dirt road, until there was nothing to watch anymore, and we went back inside.

Chapter 16

~~~~~~

Occasionally, Culphert would allow me and my brother to spend a weekend with Uncle Lofton and Aunt Amanda. Aunt Amanda would cook our favorite dishes as she had when we lived with them. We would say our prayers with Uncle Lofton and go to bed.

One morning I awoke to hear Aunt Amanda running through the house screaming, "Oh, Lord! He's dead!" I didn't know what was going on, but I knew that something terrible had happened. Was Uncle Lofton dead? The notion shot through me like electricity.

The door opened and Uncle Lofton appeared. "Get dressed, we going to Carver's Creek. Eveline just killed Jack!"

We scrambled into our clothes and were in the car in no time. Aunt Amanda was screaming and crying, "She killed Jack!" Jack was her oldest brother.

I remembered him well, for when we lived with Aunt Amanda and Uncle Lofton, we visited them frequently. He and Eveline had eight children. When we went to visit with them, we played with our cousins until we had to leave. They were my closest friends during those years.

Carver's Creek, a township at the foot of the Oakland Plantation, was where my father's people were from. Since the Civil War, our people came from that swampy area. Uncle Jack, like his other sisters and brothers, had built a house not far from where he was born. And like the black men before him, he was a farmer.

I remembered him as taller and blacker than my father. He

145

worked hard, raised his children, and was liked by the other farmers. Like my father, he was handsome, with the typical Brown features of dark skin and aquiline nose.

That Sunday morning when we drove into the yard, there were a few cars, a few people, no police. The door was opened and just as we got out of the car, one of the girls came running out. "Mamma killed Daddy!"

We went inside the house and walked through the living room to the bedroom. Somebody had forgotten to close the window and a white curtain blew in from the outside. Lying there on the bed, facedown, was Uncle Jack. The story was that he had come home from his Saturday night prowl and fallen asleep. Eveline, crazy with jealousy, had loaded the shotgun with double-O buckshot and sneaked up behind him while he slept and killed him. "He never knew what happened," said one of the men standing in the yard.

Some people said that Eveline wouldn't get any time for killing Uncle Jack, because he was a black man and the white men in power didn't care. Eveline was sentenced to no more than a couple of years in prison and was released, went north, and this left a bitterness in the family. Still, Aunt Amanda encouraged her brother's children to visit her and ask for help, and they did. They all became very good friends and she responded to them with kindness and sympathy.

This brutal murder regurgitated the family history, and something dreadful swept over me, changing my life. Uncle Jack's death forced me to realize that there was something different about our family than those of my friends. There was violence and cruelty in the Brown family.

After we came back from Uncle Jack's funeral, Uncle Lofton, seeing how upset I was, asked me what was wrong. I told him that I didn't want to live with Culphert and Dorothy any longer.

"One day Dorothy will kill Culphert just like Eveline did Uncle Jack," I told him. "Or else Culphert will kill her."

"That's how the Browns are," he said. "Fighting and jealousy."

"But Daddy, I don't want it to happen to me!"

"Morris, you got to try to break that chain."

"But how, Uncle Lofton?" I asked him.

"You got to leave from around here," he said. "You got to get above that family."

146

"Daddy, I want to be a magician," I said. I really believed I could be a famous magician. Famous and rich. I could do whatever I wanted to do.

"You can be one if you put your heart to it," Uncle Lofton said.

I looked at the talent show on television. Why couldn't I be on the talent show? I would be able to escape the violence that was waiting for me in this family and in this little town.

I told the idea to Randell, and he agreed to go with me to Wilmington where the talent show was broadcast. For weeks, I gathered up my magic tricks into a fifteen-minute format. We would not tell anybody about what we were going to do. When they saw us on television, they would be amazed. Not that many black people had televisions, but I was driven by the idea that Uncle Lofton and Aunt Amanda, or Mamma, might see us on Uncle Lofton's television. People would talk about seeing us, and Culphert would hear about it. He might even see the show himself—and he would then see how unfair and brutal he had been to me.

The day to make the trip arrived. It was a Saturday, and we met that morning at the old railroad station near the train tracks. I knew the 11:55 came through because Uncle Lofton worked on the railroad. Even though Randell knew when the train came through also, I felt I was the real authority on the railroad because of Uncle Lofton's association with the Atlantic Coast Line.

"But you sure the train is going to stop for us?" Randell asked as we walked across the tracks.

"Yeah, I use to see Daddy wave it down," I said, "and I know how to do it." When my brother and I were small we had witnessed Uncle Lofton's waving the train down with his red handkerchief many times. There was a special way to wave which was an official gesture that would make the engineer stop. And although the train had ceased making a stop in Bolton for many years now, I knew I could do it.

Randell and I saw the train, a small black dot, coming in the distance. We waited as the train grew larger and larger until its black thundering iron presence was upon us. When it was about a mile off, along Gramma Commie's house, I pulled out the red handkerchief and began waving it the way I had seen Uncle Lofton do when he was instructed by A. J. Harris to stop the train.

"Is it gonna stop?" Randell yelled beside me.

147

I watched it as it came up to me without slackening its speed. It was close enough for me to see the engineer's white face and the blue railroad cap. We stood back as the engine blasted by us. The wind from the engine blew us into one another. I gripped my magic bag as the steam discharged from the pistons, accompanied by a shrieking, ear-piercing whistle.

Randell looked at me. The train was actually slowing down! I glanced down the line of cars and saw a black man in a red cap leaning out from between the cars. The look of surprise on his face became clearer as the train brought him up to us.

The train finally stopped, and the man was standing right in front of us.

"Get on! Get on!" he yelled at us. We were glued to the ground until he yelled at us to hurry up. Putting my foot on the steel step, I grabbed the thin iron railing and pulled myself and my magic bag onto the train.

"Okay, okay, let's go," he said to Randell, who came right behind me. "It's been a long time since somebody flagged this train down! Now, where you boys going?"

"Wilmington," I said. "We going to Wilmington."

"Now what you gonna do in Wilmington," he said, looking at us suspiciously. "You boys ain't running away from homes, is you?"

"No, we going to be on the talent show," I told him. "We're magicians."

"What?"

"We gonna be on television," I said.

"On television," he said, looking first at me and then at Randell. "Now, does you mamma and daddy know you going to be on television?"

"No," I told him, "we are going to surprise them. The talent show comes on at four o'clock. And when they look at the talent show, they'll be surprised to see us."

"Oh, I see," he said, looking around at the white people who sat down in the nice seats. Then he said, "Listen, you boys come with me."

He took us to another section of the train where the colored people sat and told us to sit down and look out the window.

"Do we have to buy a ticket?"

"No, don't worry about that." He smiled. "You just sit right there and look out the window and enjoy your trip. I'll be right back and talk to you both when I have time."

We sat by the window and watched the fields fly by. I had been to Wilmington so many times that I knew every speck of the scenery, and yet it was exciting to see it all from a train. We passed Acme, and Delco, the town that marked the boundary of Uncle Lofton's work on the railroad.

Occasionally we checked the goldfish to see how he was making it. He was concealed in a small tube under my coat. To perform the goldfish trick, I asked for an empty glass of water, and after having the audience examine it (sometimes I drank from it to prove that there was nothing fishy about it), I placed a white pocket handkerchief, which I also borrowed from the audience, over it. Then I said a few magic words and pulled the pocket handkerchief off the glass of water. They were astonished to see a live goldfish swimming around in the glass.

Such a trick, I thought as I watched the Wilmington bridge looming in the distance, would astonish anybody. Surely these white people at the talent show were no different from the white people who had seen my tricks before. They would be amazed by my tricks as everybody else had been.

The train roared across the bridge. We looked down and saw the steamboats and tugboats below. Farther ahead of us was the city of Wilmington, so large, so shining. It was the greatest city in the whole world.

"Y'all know where the television station is?" the conductor asked us, as the train pulled into the station.

"Oh yessir! On Fourth Street and Front!"

When he asked us what kind of talent we had, I offered to show him a trick. I took a quarter out and made it disappear, and that astonished him. Then I reached up and pulled it out of his ear. He was amazed, just like all the others.

When we disembarked from the train, he took us to the train station and out to the street. "Now you boys be good," he said. "And good luck on being on that television station." We told him we would, and he kept waving at us as we left.

We found the television station and told the woman at the desk we were there for the talent show.

"You here for the what?" she said. "What you here fer?" She was a blond-haired woman, a gum-chewing woman. I told her

CECIL BROWN

again. She said just a minute and called somebody on the telephone, glaring at us as she told them about us.

A man came out and took us to the back. We came into a room
with television cameras.

"You boys are here for the talent show?"

"Yes, sir."

"What kind of talent do you have? You sing?"

"No, sir," I explained. "I'm a magician and this is James Randell, my assistant."

"Is that so?" he said, just like he didn't believe me.

"Yessir," I said. "We perform magic shows all the time."

"Where do you perform your shows? In school?"

"Yessir!"

"Have you seen our show?"

"Every Saturday!"

"Do you see what kind of people we have on our show?" he
asked.

"Yes, sir." I didn't know what he was saying. I had seen the
other kids on the show. They were baton-whirling girls, hillbilly
singers, and square dancers. I had never seen a magician act. So
I knew I would be the first magician they would have on the show.

"And so you know that we don't have certain kinds of people
on the show, don't you?"

"No, sir!" I said, still not understanding him.

"Do you want to see some of our tricks?" Randell asked.

"Well, I don't know. It makes no sense for you boys to do your
tricks now, because . . . we have a policy," he said. Then, looking
at us again, he said, "Well, what kind of tricks do you do?"

"Could I borrow your cigarette?" I asked him. He looked at the
cigarette he was smoking and handed it to me. I took it with my
right hand and formed a cup with my left hand. Then I stuffed
the burning cigarette into my cupped hand and squeezed it, and
slowly unfolded my hand, revealing it to be empty.

"That's . . . very . . . uh good, boys!"

"We do a complete magic act from three minutes to fifteen
minutes," I explained. "Do you want to see us do some more?"

He rubbed his head and looked puzzled. "Well, uh, let me get
somebody else to watch this," he said, and turned to another man.
"Say, Doug, we got some colored kids here. Magicians."

Doug was a tall, skinny man with glasses.

"What is it?"

150

"These kids are good!" the first man said. "Should we make a tape of their act?"

Doug came over to us. "So you boys want to be on television, huh?"

"Yes, sir."

He looked at me.

"What kind of magic do you do?" he asked.

"I disappear things," I explained. "Like your necktie . . ."

The first man cut in. "Give him a cigarette, Doug, and let's see what he does with it."

I never do a trick the second time to the same audience, so I picked another one. "Do you have a dollar bill? We do a telepathy trick that people like."

Looking suspicious, Doug took out his wallet and handed me a crinkled-up dollar bill. While he was taking it out, I took out a white handkerchief and tied it around Randell's eyes. We had done this trick many times before for the PTA meetings at my school, and I knew how impressed adults were with mental telepathy tricks. I took the dollar bill and folded it and pressed it to my forehead.

"Okay, Randell, please concentrate . . . Now, think of the numbers on the bill . . . Are you ready?"

"I'm ready," Randell said.

"Now what is on the bill. What year is it issued?"

"Nineteen-fifty," Randell said.

I handed the bill to Doug so that he could verify the date.

Unfolding it, he smiled and said, "That's right!"

"Now, Randell, tell us the serial number of the bill."

The white men looked at the bill together, while Randell read out the serial number. ". . . Eleven, five, two, seven, eight, seven, zero, seven, four, dee . . ."

"That's pretty good, boys," Doug said, shaking his head.

"Now will you let us be on television?" I asked him.

He took a deep breath, shook his head, and looked at his partner again.

"This breaks my heart, but . . ." he said, and then, looking at the other man yet another time. "Okay, Fred, let's make a videotape of them."

"But you know that's not the policy!" Fred said. "We can't break the policy on this issue."

"Just set it up for them to go on next," he said, and then he turned to us. "Get ready! We're going to film you. Now, you know how television works, don't you? We film the show and we run it a few weeks later."

"It won't come on television today at four o'clock?" I asked. I thought that all television was live.

"No, we will show it two or three weeks later," he said. "And we will tell you when. Now, you fellows get ready."

We went into the bathroom and prepared the goldfish in a small tube hidden under my long coat. Then we prepared the milk pitcher, pouring milk into a false-bottomed pitcher. In ten minutes we were ready.

We were brought out in front of the television camera. I was nervous, but as soon as the man behind the camera said, "Okay, go!" I lost all of my inhibitions.

"Ladies and gentlemen . . ." I said, launching into my spiel. I performed my first trick and heard somebody clap their hands. Then I went into the next one. This required me to punch a hole into Randell's head with a knife and catch the milk that ran out of his head. We ended with the goldfish trick. When we were finished, everybody was applauding.

"Very good," Fred said. "That was terrific, boys!"

He made us come to his office.

"Now, boys, we're going to call you and tell you when the show's coming on the air, okay?" We had to give him our names and addresses.

"That was a great pleasure having you audition for the talent show," he said, shooing us to the door. "Good-bye!"

As we were leaving the building, a white woman came up to us.

"That was terrible and cruel of them to do that to you boys," she said. "And you were so good too!"

"To do what to us?" I asked her.

"I work at that television station," she said, "and I think it was a disgrace for them to pretend that they were going to use you on the show."

"But I don't understand?"

"They told you they would have you on the show, but that was a lie. They said that just to get rid of you. We have a policy not to have colored people on the show. And they didn't tell you that, did they?"

I felt disappointed. It must have shown in my face, because she leaned over.

"Listen, you fellows are very good. Don't let this discourage you! But they didn't have the guts to tell you that they are not going to use you. It's too bad! But don't let that stop you, do you understand? You could vanish cigarettes, change the colors of silk handkerchiefs, produce goldfish out of thin air." She laughed. "But you couldn't change the color of your skin! If you could do that, you might have a chance! Well, good luck and don't be discouraged." She walked off down the street.

As we made our way back to the train station, I still couldn't believe it. But we were good, weren't we? Didn't they all say we were good?

"Well," I said to Randell, as the train pulled out of Wilmington. "We were almost on television, weren't we?"

"Yeah," he laughed, "almost . . ."

That next week I watched the show, still hoping to see us, but we didn't appear. Maybe we would be on the next week . . . I watched the next week and the week following that . . . and the week following that . . . We were never on it.

Chapter 17

"Whoa!" I yelled and pulled back on the black leather lines. The two jet black mules reared and jerked the wagon Knee and I rode on.

We were coming out of the gate of our new home, the Hill Farm, a big white house perched on the top of a steep clay hill. My sisters Brenda Faye and Vivian Ann, and the baby of the family, Frederick Ethan, were born on the Hill Farm. Realizing that he couldn't make enough money on the Green Swamp farm to support our growing family, Culphert took a sharecropping arrangement from a white woman, Bertha Long. We were headed to her place to pick up a plow. Culphert had made us hitch up the two mules to a double-tree wagon, our first time doing anything like this.

The two mules were twins called Pat and Mike. They were the nastiest, meanest animals I had ever encountered. Unlike Big Red, these two short, fat demons were contrary and rebellious. But since we were sharecropping for her, Bertha Long insisted that we use them. We hadn't been living on the Hill Farm two weeks before a white neighbor woke Culphert up one morning complaining that those "durn" mules were eating his corn. Knee and I had to run through the dewy cornfield, catch them, bring them back, and lock them in, only to find that they had broken out again and were found back in that white man's cornfield.

I slapped the leather lines on their shiny black rumps with revengeful licks.

As the wagon rolled along the highway toward Bertha Long's

house, I looked to my right side at Walter Davis's spacious farm. Walter Davis and his wife and three boys were our neighbors.

Already Knee and I had encountered the Davis boys. When I was alone, the two older ones caught me and called me a name and threatened to beat me up. Knee and I waited until we caught the small one alone in the back field. I made him fight Knee, telling him that if he beat my brother, I was going to beat him. He was trembling with fright as we piled on him and bloodied his nose. It was a law that if they caught us alone they would do the same.

Across the mailbox, on the other side of the road, were our other neighbors, Henry Lomax, his wife Helen, and their little girl, Jill, who was about my age. My mother and Helen picked berries together, canned fruits, and visited each other. They were, as it turned out, close friends. She and Helen had grown up close together and had known each other from childhood.

The Hill Farm was located three miles outside of Bolton. We had moved from a black farm into an integrated farming community. There was a real barn, like the kind you see in the *Progressive Farmer's Journal*, complete with a hayloft from which the animals could easily be fed. As the school bus drove into our new farm, I was actually proud of it. It looked like a rich white person's farm.

As we drove the double mule team up to Bertha Long's place, we noticed on her front lawn two Sambo statues, which my brother and I detested. They were grinning, red-lipped nigger statues holding up plants.

When I was a child my uncle and aunt would take my brother and me for rides in their car, and when we passed one of these statues, they would say, "Look, there's Cornelius! And look"—if there were two statues—"Morris with him!" The white people would have these symbols of denigration stuck on their front lawns like gargoyles to ward off evil rebellious Negro spirits. Whites thought they were really something when they had one of these ugly things stuck near the doorsteps.

We passed the white flat house which had awls on the windows and as we passed the gate, we saw another such statue on the back porch.

Bertha herself, flat-faced, manly woman, was straddling her tractor in the field. She turned the tractor around and came up to the barn where we were loading the plow onto the wagon. She

155

patted Mike and Pat just like they were her children, and after saying a few words to us left us alone. As soon as we were out of the gate, we started beating those two mules as if we were going to kill them. When we got back to the farm, they were panting so hard, I thought they would drop dead. I hated those two neurotic mules.

Culphert often talked about how with the tractor and the two mules, we didn't need Big Red, hinting that he wanted to sell her. But I didn't want Big Red to be sold, because she was my only friend. I figured that if Culphert saw me plowing her in the garden, he would see her usefulness. So every evening after I'd fed up the animals and milked the cows, I'd take Big Red out and plow in Dorothy's garden with her, so that I could prove that we needed her.

One evening, as I was plowing, I saw a car turning up into the gate. I didn't know who it was, for I'd never seen that car before, yet it looked familiar.

When I got back to the end of the row, I heard a strange sound coming from the house, like a cat's yowling. After a while, I saw Knee running from the house.

"Morris, come quick! Culphert wants you!"

Tying up Big Red, I went up to the house, around to the porch. Seated on the porch was Mr. McNeil, the new music teacher from school. I had completely forgotten that he was going to come by and talk to our parents.

"Hello, Brown," Mr. McNeil said.

"Hello," I muttered, embarrassed that Culphert was there.

"Morris, I'm demonstrating the saxophone sound to your parents," Mr. McNeil said. "So take a seat and I'll continue."

A week earlier Mr. Corbett, the principal of our high school, a flamboyant man in his early thirties and an immaculate dresser who sported a part down the middle of his conked head and a white cigarette holder clinched between a set of pearl teeth, told us that he was going to start a marching band. He introduced this new teacher, who stated that if anybody wanted to join the music class, they were welcome to do so. During the class he brought out a number of instruments and tried them out for us. He played the trombone and then the saxophone and the trumpet.

I took up the sax and fingered the keys up and down a few times.

"Do you like that instrument?" the new teacher asked me.

"I guess so," I replied.

"Try to blow something out of it," he demanded.

Putting it to my lips, I blew with all my might. The sound that came out was like a fart. Leon laughed and tried to do it. He got another fart sound.

"Great, great," Mr. McNeil said, obviously encouraging us. After we had all tried a couple of instruments, he turned to the class.

"Now we don't have any money to buy these instruments," he said. "These are my own private ones. Some of them belong to my brothers. But if we are serious about being musicians, we have to have instruments. Now I'm going to ask those of you who are interested to raise your hands."

Leon, Randell, Kenneth, and Dorothy Lyons and I raised our hands.

"Very good," he said. "Now, in order to get these instruments, we're going to have to persuade your parents to buy instruments for us. The way we do this is the same way I did with you. I'll play a few instruments for your parents and then after I'm gone, you can put the final touch on them."

After school that day on the bus, we all talked about the band with each other. "I think my daddy will let me buy a baritone," Randell said. Randell had a great daddy, very warm and understanding. Whenever I went to their house, he was always in a white shirt reading the papers. He was a laborer, but he wanted his sons and daughters to go to college.

"Yeah, my daddy will let me get that saxophone," Leon said. "I heard him talking about it already."

Kenneth turned to me. "What about you, Morris? You think Cuffy gonna let you get a saxophone?"

I hung my head. I knew without a doubt that Culphert was going to pitch a bitch if I even mentioned him spending any money on me. I was simply not worth it in his eyes.

But now as Mr. McNeil played the saxophone, Culphert's eyes lit up with pleasure. He asked me if I wanted to play it, and I said I did, knowing that he wouldn't buy it for me.

Culphert shook hands with Mr. McNeil and told him to have the music man come by with a selection of saxophones.

A few days later, when I came back from milking the cow, Mamma said to me, "Culphert said the music man is here."

"Why?" I asked.

The only reason he would want the music man to come by would be to humiliate me further. And then when the music man, who was bound to be white, had shown off all the instruments, Culphert would raise a storm about how expensive they were and how much I was asking him to spend on me.

When I got up to the house, the white man had a half dozen cases of instruments opened on the porch. He was a thin, blond-haired man. He didn't play the instruments like Mr. McNeil did, just talked a good talk and I doubted that he could even play one of them. When he got to a particular instrument, all he did was flex the valves or pump the slide. When it was decided that I wanted a saxophone, he showed us three.

One was used and the other two were new. Of the two new saxophones, I liked the silver one, but I was afraid to say anything. I wasn't at all sure that Culphert would even let me play one, let alone buy one for me.

The music salesman was making his pitch, and his best opportunity was to persuade me to pick out one I liked. He handed me the used saxophone.

"Feel how comfortable it is," he said to me as I held it.

"Do you like it?" my father asked.

"Yes, sir," I said.

I wanted the new one, the brand-new one, but I pointed to the used one because I thought this would be the one he would buy. Anybody who was as mean as he was to me wasn't about to buy me a brand-new instrument.

"What's wrong with that one?" Culphert asked me, pointing to the new shiny one.

"Nothing," I said, not believing that he was serious about it.

"Now, if I buy you this thing, you gonna play it," he said.

"Yes, sir!"

"Okay," he said to the salesman. "We'll take that one."

"You want this one," the white man said, and he gave me another look. I couldn't believe that Culphert was talking about the new instrument. I didn't know what it cost, but it must have cost a lot.

"That's right," Culphert said, as if he was ready to start a fight with the man. "I want that one! Is that the best one you got?"

"That's the top of the line," he said.

"Okay, give me that one. And the case, too."

When the salesman was gone, I carried the instrument to my room. I couldn't get used to the idea that I had a new horn.

When I took the horn to school the next day, I was proud, especially when I opened the case in the band room. Everybody gathered around it and wanted to hold it or blow in the mouthpiece. Mr. McNeil called the class to order.

"Now I want to show you all something," he said, and went to the blackboard and drew the chromatic scale. "I want all of you to copy this down and go home and practice it. Practice it until you have mastered it."

I turned and looked about the classroom. There were twenty other students with instruments. Most of them, like my buddies Kenneth and Leon, held used instruments which their parents had bought. But I was the only one with a brand-new horn. I should have thanked Culphert for that, but I was still so afraid of him that I didn't know how I should feel about his generosity.

"All of the girls who want to try out to be majorettes," McNeil said, "will meet us outside after class." He looked over the class and then said, "Now those of you who have permission from your parents to practice with us after school also meet us after class at the back of the schoolhouse."

I wished I had permission from Culphert to stay after school, because I wanted to practice very much, and because the girls who were to be majorettes were very beautiful. Leon and Kenneth, who didn't have to work on the farm as I did, stayed after school to practice. I was determined that I would ask Culphert if I could practice too, but I was a bit apprehensive about it because I thought he had done a lot by buying me the saxophone.

When I came home that day, I took the saxophone up to the hayloft to practice my scales. When I blew my first big note, the cows came running from the field, the chickens ran for cover, the dogs barked, the black mules jittered nervously, and the crows cawed. I practiced for about an hour in the hayloft, with nobody to bother me but the farm animals.

"Boy, what's wrong with these animals," I heard Culphert yelling to me. I went to the barn door and saw him standing down on the ground.

"I don't know," I said.

" 'I don't know,' " he said, mocking me. "You scaring these mules and chickens and things with that noise." But he wasn't mad; he

159

was actually laughing a bit. Culphert was in such a good mood about the music I was playing that I thought it was safe to ask him if I could get permission to stay after school to practice.

"Come down here and help me," he called. I rushed down the steps after carefully putting my horn in the purple-velvet-lined case.

When I came down I saw that he had taken the wheel from the wagon. Taking the axle, I held it up while he applied globs of axle grease on the hub.

"Culphert," I started cautiously, "if I work hard today, milk the cow and feed up before the school bus comes, can I stay after school to practice with the band?"

"You make sure that all of your work is done, and I reckon you can."

The answer surprised me. I was so happy that I wanted to shout, but I remained passive, reserving my excitement until I could share it with Leon, Kenneth, and Randell. I knew that it was a great sacrifice for him to let me stay after school because he needed me on the farm.

I began staying after school and practicing with the band.

Mr. McNeil began to teach us to march the way he had learned from the famed A & T marching band. Immediately he recognized our greatest asset: all of these country boys and girls were in great physical shape. Our muscular bodies allowed us to march for miles without the slightest bit of exhaustion. Having grown up in a city, Mr. McNeil had never seen anything quite like it.

During our music hour, instead of sitting in the classroom practicing scales like most high school students, we marched three miles to the highway 74–76 and three miles back blowing our instruments all the way. As we marched through the farm areas, people working in the fields would stop and lean on their hoes, watching us with pride and delight. Dogs barked at our shoes and children stood in amazement.

Not long after, we gave our first concert in the school gymnasium. Our opening tune was "St. Louis Blues," and we played it with gusto. Mr. McNeil and Mr. Corbett stood proudly by as our parents listened to us with a new sense of local dignity.

A donation was taken up for our uniforms and the parents complied to this demand as Mr. Corbett had predicted they would. When we got our new uniforms, we were thrilled. Our colors were maroon and gold and we became the stars of the high school.

Mr. Corbett's idea of a flashy marching band was to attract the parents to the wonderful things that the high school could do. Since Armour High was, even by black standards in North Carolina, dirt poor, there was no money for football equipment, so there was no football team. If we were too poor to have a football team, then at least we could have a marching band. The parents would see their sons and daughters marching up and down the country roads, hear the playing, and would realize what a great difference their dimes and pennies had made to bring this about.

Music soon became one of the two ways I could enjoy any semblance of freedom. Whenever I wanted to go somewhere, I'd say to Culphert, "If I work hard today, could I go to band practice tomorrow?" Culphert'd say something like, "You make sure that all your work has been finished before you go, and I reckon you can." Sometimes, Leon Lloyd and James Randell would bring their instruments and get off the bus at my house and we would practice in the hay barn. Leon played saxophone, James Randell played baritone horn, and Kenneth Melvin, trumpet. At other times, I would meet them at school and we would practice together.

Mr. McNeil gave us a copy of "St. Louis Blues" and showed us how to transpose the music from one instrument to another. We didn't have enough money to buy music sheets, so we would take one piece and transpose it for different instruments. If we got a piece of music in bass, we would transpose it into treble for the other instruments. While transposing "Sha-boom!" we got the idea to start our own band, the Bebop Kings.

That spring, Mr. McNeil announced to us during the music class that we had received an invitation to be in the Strawberry Festival. In order to bring our musical skills up to par with the other schools before we participated, Mr. McNeil took us to Raleigh, the state capital, about three hundred miles away.

When we got there, we were divided up and placed in groups according to the instrument we played. After several hours of practicing, we had to give recitals, which were listened to attentively. From this recital, the instructors picked a few students from each group to form a band which would then play for all the students.

Mr. McNeil passed the saxophone room where he opened the door to listen to what was going on. As he opened the door, he saw me standing in front of the class giving my recital. He noticed that as I played, I made jazz riffs which seemed to annoy the instructor.

After the recital, he noticed that I had a sad look on my face because I wasn't one of those chosen to form the band. But some of the fellows who had been chosen were up in arms about the fact that the instructor hadn't chosen me.

They said that because I played my riff so well the rest of the exercises didn't matter. They all wanted me to play with the band.

"Brown, you know you have an incredible influence over people," Mr. McNeil said to me as we were driving home. He was impressed that I had made the guys like me so well that they were ready to fight for me after having known me for only an hour. He was impressed by what most people noticed about me at that time, which was my ability to get people to like me.

Chapter 18

━━━━━━━━━━━━━━━━━━━━━━━━━━━━━━━━━━━

As the band prepared for the Strawberry Festival in the spring, I had time enough for my other classes. I had algebra from Dr. Robinson, English and French from Miss Laws, music from Miss White, home economics, a class we boys took because all the pretty girls were in it, from Miss Claybrook, and agriculture and carpentry from Mr. Adams.

One day I saw a student wearing a shiny jacket with the letters "NFA" across the pocket. When I learned that members of the New Farmers of America got those jackets, I wanted to join that organization. James Randell, Leon Lloyd, Kenneth Melvin, and I decided that these jackets were the coolest things happening, and we had to have one.

In his class Mr. Adams introduced those students who were interested to the New Farmers of America, which was a competitive club that traveled to other towns to compete in livestock judging contests, talent shows, and parliamentary procedure.

"This federation New Farmers of America," he explained to us that fall day in 1957, "is a member of the R. Taylor Federation. They raise money to support young girls and boys at the Oxford Orphanage. Now those of you who have parents can do something good for those who don't. Join the NFA and all the money we make will be sent to the orphanage."

The R. Taylor Federation? Oxford Orphanage? We were bored stiff with all this long-winded stuff! What about the jackets?

"We will travel to all eight schools that are in the federation. Those are Shilot, Pender County, Hallsboro, Whiteville, Tabor City, East Arcadia, Hallsboro, and Burgaw."

All these schools were black, and we were anxious to see what they were like, but what about the jackets?

"We want to get ourselves some of these NFA jackets," Mr. Adams said, finally getting to the point. "And to do that, I want each of you to bring fifteen dollars to school." He then passed around the NFA jacket, which was made of some kind of shiny material with a big NFA over the left pocket.

As I walked through the gate to the farm that afternoon, I wondered how I was going to get that fifteen dollars from Culphert. When I was living with Uncle Lofton, I would sell shoes from a mail-order company to make money, or in the spring I would sell seeds, but Culphert never gave me the extra time to do anything like that. There was always too much work to do at the farm.

As the weeks went by we were obliged to attend Mr. Adams's lectures on livestock. When Mr. Adams would show us pictures of a Duroc or a spotted Poland China or a Berkshire, I would rush home to the Hill Farm and go out to the pigpen and actually look at a spotted Poland China. When he showed us pictures of different kinds of cows and chickens, I'd go home and go into the pasture and examine the type that was listed in the agriculture book.

Our farm became, in this way, a living laboratory. I became such an expert at looking at a pig that I could even guess the age, weight, and size of a litter even before they were born. There were four kinds of pigs—feeders, bolders, gilts, and sows—and many different breeds. By looking at the arch in the back, length of the body, the lucidness or brightness in the eyes, the thickness of the hair, I could tell if a pig was healthy or sick, fertile or sterile.

One afternoon while feeding the pigs, I noticed that some of the barrows were looking strange around the eyes. Mr. Adams had said that a barrow should "stand up good and look alert about the eyes," but I could tell that our barrows didn't.

Barrows are young male pigs that have been castrated before they are old enough to mate with a gilt (a female pig before she has her first litter). We had castrated them about a month ago. I had dreaded this activity, but it had to be done. We had caught them, tied their hind legs and pulled their sacs tight, and cut out their balls and doused the wound with kerosene.

I went around to the end of the pigs and looked at the rear ends where the knife had deprived them of their sexual organs. It looked swollen. I saw that something was moving in the wound. Worms, I realized suddenly, the pigs had become infested with ringworms. I went to the house and told Culphert. Not long ago an epidemic had broken out in Walter Davis's pigs and killed about fifty of them. I knew that if Culphert was able to prevent such an epidemic from breaking out among our pigs, he would save a lot of money. I would be a hero.

"How do you know that?" he asked me.

"The barrows supposed to look alert," I said, with a certain authority, "but they don't."

"Who told you that?"

"That's what we learn in NFA."

"What's that?"

"New Farmers of America," I said.

"Uh-huh!" he sighed, and then, as he moved from the chair, he barked a laugh. I followed him to the barn, where he leaned over the fence and studied the pigs.

"Damn," he said, "those pigs *do* have worms."

He got medicine for them from Bertha Long. My brother and I had to help him put it on the pigs. When we were finished, I said, "Culphert, I need fifteen dollars to buy my jacket for the New Farmers of America."

"What you need that for?"

"I want to go on a trip with them."

"Who said you could go some damn where?"

"But don't you see? The more knowledge I have about the farm, the more I can help *you*. If I didn't know what to look for in the pigs, you wouldn't have known about the worms until it was too late. That would have cost you the life of maybe twenty pigs."

I could sense that he was thinking about the epidemic that nearly ruined Walter Davis.

"Why can't you go on the trip without a jacket?" he asked, but I could tell from the look on his face that he was going to let me have the jacket.

"Everybody else got one," I said, watching him go into his overalls pocket and come out with the money.

"Now here," he said, "I don't want to hear no mo bout this damn New Farmers of America, you hear me, boy!"

"Yes, sir!" I grinned as he laid the money in my hand. This was

165

a solid triumph for me. I went to my room with a big smile on my face. Finally, I had been able to deal with him! The best way to deal with Culphert was to outthink him.

The NFA club turned out to be my best opportunity to get away from home. We traveled through the school year to other towns. We went to Hallsboro where, because of a large selection of beef, the cattle-judging competition was held; to Tabor City where the poultry contests were held; and to Elizabeth City where the pig-judging contest was held.

When we went to Tabor City to judge pigs, we wore our new NFA jackets. As a member of the club, I specialized in livestock judging. (Needless to say, we wore our NFA jackets everywhere we went, including band practice.) We were about five in all and Mr. Adams drove us there in his car.

"Now remember, fellows," Mr. Adams said as we drove along, "there are four subject areas we are going to be judging. What are they?"

Randell said, "Beef, dairy, hens, and pigs!"

"Right," Mr. Adams said, "and with the beef what are we looking for, Lloyd?"

Leon said, "Compact, smooth, and muscular."

"Right, and what else, Brown?"

"And not showing a lot of fat," I said.

"Right," he congratulated. "And what about the dairy? What are we looking for in the dairy?"

I said, "Good quarters, milk bag must be heavy, the back must be in a good shape, short hair, and good posture."

"And hogs," he asked. "What are the main divisions in hogs, Brown?"

The hog judging was my specialty. "There are four kinds. First, the litter, which are pigs under a hundred and ten pounds. Then comes the gilt, females before they have their first litter. They must be 'active around the head,' have an arched back so that they can carry their litter well, and they must look like good producers. Now comes the barrow; they are castrated male pigs."

"Why are they castrated?" he asked me.

"Because they are going to be slaughtered."

"You only named three," he said. "What's the fourth kind?"

"The sow! The sow has to have a large arched back so that the heavy litter won't break her down."

166

"Okay," he said, as the car pulled into the small town and we turned to watch the passersby.

"Now Kenneth Melvin is not here," Mr. Adams reminded us. Kenneth Melvin was our expert on hens and chickens, but he was sick. "Who's going take his place?"

I liked Kenneth and felt obligated to fill in for his absence because we had grown up together.

"I'll take his place," I said.

"When you're judging a hen, how can you tell how many eggs she is producing?"

I had been around chickens all my life and yet I didn't know.

"Tell me before I get there," I said to him.

"Take the hen and run your finger under her pelvis and feel the empty sack. If it is large, she will produce about a dozen in two days. If it's small, about half that amount."

"What is large? And small?"

"A large sac is about the size of your fist," he said, as we got out of the car.

We milled around the farm, meeting people and drinking sodas until the competition began.

I took my placard and number and put it on my jacket and walked up to the pen.

"Okay," the judge said, "you have ten minutes."

I walked over to the first pig and saw immediately that it was a spotted Poland China. I judged him to be fair, but not excellent. Then I went on to a Berkshire, which was excellent. When I finished I turned my cards in to the judge and went on to the beef competition.

When we finished, Mr. Adams said, "We have placed number one in judging the livestock. We are going to get the first-prize trophy."

But what was even more important, I found the hard life of being a farmer's son alleviated by the ability to attach words and values to previously mundane surroundings. It opened up a whole new world for me.

Chapter 19

In 1959, I was sixteen, and the leader of my own rhythm and blues band, the Bebop Kings. There was me on the sax, Leon on Trombone, Randell on bass (he turned a tin washtub over and put a broom handle with a piece of rope on it), Sam White the vocalist, and the piano player, O'Neil Richardson.

We played in JC Himes's place on Saturday nights. JC would give us forty dollars and all the free corn liquor we could drink. Culphert came into JC's one night when we were playing but left immediately. He didn't like for me to play music and told me sometime later, "You should be working more in the field."

I heard somebody telling him, "Man, that boy of yours can play!" But Culphert said nothing. I couldn't understand how he had bought me the instrument and then didn't like that I was good on it.

While I played music through high school, I had to work in the fields after school during the spring and all day during the summer. When we weren't working our own farm, my brother and I would work for other people in the field. One of these people was Henry Lomax, who had the big farm across the road.

One day I went to work with some other guys in Henry Lomax's field cropping tobacco. As the drag got to the end of the row, we were at the back yard of Henry Lomax's house. Jill, his sixteen-year-old daughter, was hanging the clothes out on the line. We were close enough to her to speak to her, but we were quiet instead. But as soon as we had worked back down to the other end of the field, way out of hearing, Leon stood up.

168

"Hey, Pyatt," he said, "how is it?"

"How's what?"

"Nigger, we know you been gettin that stuff."

"What stuff?"

"Pyatt been over there gettin that white stuff," Leon laughed. "But he won't say nothin."

"Aw, gon and leave me lone," Pyatt said.

Leon said that Pyatt was screwing Jill Lomax, but Pyatt was silent, naturally not admitting any such thing. Then why was he always over there working in the fields, if something wasn't going on? Leon wanted to know. Pyatt said he needed the work. And besides, Pyatt went on, everybody knew that Henry Lomax was a Ku Klux. Pyatt said he wasn't that crazy. He didn't want to get strung up by the Ku Klux.

Leon's suggestion that Jill Lomax would sleep with Pyatt enraged me with jealousy. Whenever we came to the end of the field, I looked over at her finishing hanging up the clothes, looked at her beautiful white features, her long, black hair and shapely figure.

I was secretly in love with Jill and considered it an intrusion that Pyatt was even mentioned in the same sentence with her. After all, I was Jill's nearest neighbor.

When my mother used to visit Helen, my brother and I were left to play with Jill. She must have been thirteen then, and I was about fourteen. We were not aware of race or sex. I just knew that she was beautiful and that she loved to play tag with me.

One evening we played until it was time to go home. Jill put her hand on the car door and instead of tagging it, I kissed her hand. She giggled and I put my hand on the door and she kissed mine.

As we played this revised version of tag, my mother realized that something strange was going on. She was too polite to stop us and so we continued to touch and kiss each other's hands. But when we were in the car on the way home, Dorothy slapped me across the face.

"What you hit me for?" I asked, astonished. She had never had the nerve to hit me before.

"You know you better not get fresh with that girl," she said firmly.

I didn't know what getting "fresh" meant, but I thought it had something to do with Jill being white. Of course, I knew that my being black limited my involvement with whites, but I didn't know that restriction applied to white women and girls. Now my mother was teaching me with a backhand slap that it was forbidden, impressing upon me how dangerous it was and reminding me of the story of Emmett Till, the black boy who was lynched because he whistled at a white woman.

Still, it was difficult to keep apart, especially since we played gigs at places like the Smith's Anchorage Club.

And when we played there, it wasn't until we took our stand on the bandstand that I realized that we were playing for a white high school dance. As I gave the downbeat to the band, we brought out our theme song, "Good-Rockin' Daddy." The white school students were dressed up in their finest and seated at white-clothed tables, the ones I used to pour water and set the table for.

I had never thought about what happened to the white kids I played with when I was very little, because we went to separate high schools. Now, as we played, and as they danced, I saw them again. All the Harris boys, Bobby, and Robert were there.

"Morris! Morris Brown!" I heard somebody calling me, as I sat my horn down to take a break. As I turned I saw Jill Lomax. She was the most beautiful girl in the whole bunch. She came up to me.

"Jill," I said.

"Morris Brown," she said, as if she couldn't believe she was looking at me. What was going through her mind? I imagined that she hadn't thought about me as anything but the little black boy that tagged along with my mother.

"I know him," she said to the white boy who stood looking at her with astonishment.

"You know him?" the white boy said; I assumed he was her date. "Where do you know him from?"

"He is my neighbor," she explained, and then turned to me. "You sho can play that thing!"

"Yeah," I said, and looked at her again.

She wanted to say something to me and I wanted to say something to her, but her date pulled her away and I went out to take a cigarette break with the other fellows in the band.

As I dragged on my cigarette, I couldn't get her out of my mind. I knew that if I were white, I could have had her. I would marry her. I couldn't stop thinking about the way she looked at me. I remembered my mother's slap across the face, and the urge to hold Jill close to me grew into a fantasy.

Back on the bandstand, we had to play a slow drag and I watched her dance with that white guy. She would look at me and smile and I would smile back, but that was all I could do. Before the night was over, the white guys got drunk and started yelling at us, practically calling us niggers.

The next day, I kept wondering if things had been different, if there wasn't this taboo against mixing between the races, would I now be with Jill? But where could you do what you wanted to do? Where? In the North. In the North, you could do what you wanted, and if I was in the North, and Jill was there, we could talk as long as we wanted and no white boy could pull her away and no Dorothy would slap your face.

Early that spring, something happened in Bolton which was to change my life. My Uncle Lindsey was killed. He was coming home one night when he was hit by a car. The car was driven by a young white teenager who was drunk. He claimed that Lindsey staggered into the road. This may have been true, since Uncle Lindsey might have been drinking, but the impact of the car that hit him—he was thrown quite a long way—proved that the driver was speeding.

Although many people felt that the accident had been caused by the boy's negligence, it was difficult to bring any case against him. He was the son of the justice of the peace in Bolton.

They said that Mr. Judson offered Gramma a thousand dollars for the accident. It was like cheapening Lindsey's life by offering money for his death. This made everybody in our family sick. Lindsey was so special to me, I guess, because he was not much older than I was, and he had an attitude toward life I shared and admired. From the day Lindsey died, I didn't want to live in Bolton any longer.

One day, after band practice, I asked Mr. McNeil about the North.

When I asked certain black people about "the North," they always got a funny look on their faces, a look that was part frown and part smile, but mostly smile. Mr. McNeil had that same look on his face. "You've never been north, have you?"

"No, but I don't think I'll ever go, either," I said.

171

"Why not?" he said, frowning.

"Culphert won't let me."

"Oh, maybe he will," he said, smiling. "You could go to New York for the summer and work."

"I wish I could," I said. Then I wanted to ask him a question which I had only asked myself in the secrecy of my heart.

"Mr. McNeil, do you think I could become a famous musician if I went north?"

Mr. McNeil was not the kind of teacher who would discourage a black student, but he knew that I had only been playing a little while on the sax.

"You can do it, Brown," he said. Perhaps he was thinking of the experience at the music clinic, where I had so impressed him with my instant popularity rather than the quality of my playing. "You can do anything, man," he added, "if you just put your mind to it."

Alright, I thought, I'll put my mind to being a jazz musician. But first I had to get north.

A few days later, Mr. McNeil told me that one of the other teachers was going to New York after school finished and that I could get a ride with him and his wife. I met the teacher, Mr. Walker, who taught physical education. He told me he would be glad to give me a ride up to New York, but I would have to find somebody to stay with.

"Don't you have some relatives," he asked, "who would put you up for a summer?"

Most of the Browns or Waddells never left the area in which they were born. My family had been living in the same place since before the Civil War. For over two hundred years they lived in the same place. My mother's people only got as far as Richmond, Virginia. My mother's oldest brother, John, had gone up to Richmond to work in the shipyard and had passed for white and never came back. His brothers, Uncle Tootsie and Uncle JB, following his lead, had gone as far as Philadelphia, but I didn't want to stay with them. I wanted to be in New York City. Nothing less would do.

There was, however, a small possibility in my father's sister Eunice who had married a man called Reinze and lived with him in Harlem. (Harlem! That name made me dream of adventure.) When I lived with Uncle Lofton and Aunt Amanda, Reinze and Aunt Eunice would visit us.

172

They would drive down every year in a new car and fashionable clothes. When they went back they took a truckload of smoked cured hams and slabs of beef. In exchange, they left us stories of gangs and violence which were told to us as an indication of how miserable life in the North was. But all these stories amazed me and made me want to live in Harlem.

I rushed to Uncle Lofton and discussed the idea with him.

"Reinze and Eunice?" he said, shaking his head. "They ain't nobody for you to stay with."

"Why?"

"Man, they can't take care of themselves. How they gonna look after you?"

"But they have a new car and new clothes every year?"

"A car they pay on every month? Clothes that cover up the fact that they ain't got nothin?"

"But Daddy, I really want to go up north! Mr. McNeil said it would help me. I want to play with a real band up there and I could listen to other musicians."

Daddy said, "I ain't saying it ain't good for you." He had never been farther than Wilmington himself. But he knew that he shouldn't judge my life by his.

"What about Isaiah and Lee?" he asked me. Isaiah and Lee were very distant relatives on the Brown side. Isaiah was the second husband of my father's sister, Gertrude. When he divorced Gertty, he kept in touch with the family. His new wife was Lee, who had no connection with the Browns, but for some reason she liked the Browns—and always brought us presents.

"I trust them way more than your own people," Uncle Lofton said. I had the suspicion that Uncle Lofton felt that there was something "wrong" about the Brown blood, that there was something about the Browns that he wanted me to get away from. Often he would state it this way: "The Brown Blood don't mean the Brown's much good."

Daddy found Lee's number and called her to ask if I came up north could I stay with them? The answer was yes. I was excited. Now all I had to do was ask Culphert if it would be alright with him if I went up north for the summer. This would be the hardest part, which Uncle Lofton couldn't help me with. I had to confront Culphert myself.

Asking him if I could go up north for the summer was like the slave asking his master if he could be free. I dreaded the confrontation with him. I expressed my desire to Dorothy first.

"You better ask him," she said. "You know he's going to blow up." He would blow up. I was a valuable plowboy. He was surely going to say no.

One day, when we were alone, I finally got the nerve up to ask him.

"Culphert," I said, "I want to go up to New York and work for the summer."

"No, I need you here this summer," he said. "I want you to start breaking up that back field for the corn. And the cornfield, I want you to put the tobacco seeds there."

He didn't even take what I asked him seriously. He just assumed that I would ask him and then he would say no, and that would be the last of it.

When I was alone with Dorothy, I complained and begged her to talk to him for me. She said she would, even though she knew that he would blow up about it.

And blow up he did.

"That goddamned Lofton Freeman," he stormed on Sunday morning, "putting these stupid ideas in that boy's head! Hell no! You ain't going no goddamn where," he said to me at the table. "You better get that in your head, you hear?"

As school came to an end, the date for departure came closer and closer. Still, I hadn't talked to Culphert again about it. I was so afraid that he would beat me for asking him again. I worked in the field after school and sulked at night, not being strong enough to confront him.

I was in my eleventh year of school, and all the guys knew that I could play music, that I was a good magician, but they always teased me about my father beating me. I hated that reputation, for it made me think of myself as a child.

One day after I had put on a performance at my school, Dr. Robinson, our science teacher, told me to stay after chemistry class.

"Brown," he said, "I watched the magic show of yours." He grinned. He was a short man, but brilliant. We all called him Doctor, even though we didn't know if he had a Ph.D.

"If you can do magic shows like that," he said, "you can do anything. I think you have the ability to get a scholarship to college. Have you ever thought of going to college?"

"Yes, sir. I thought about it," I told him.

"To win a scholarship," he said, "you've got to have a good science background. Now, I'm willing to help you, if you want to work at it."

"I want to," I told him.

"Well, you'll have to work harder," he said.

"Do you think I should go work in the North for the summer?" I asked him.

"I think that would be a very good idea," he said.

My mind was made up then, for my respect for my teachers was so high that I would defy Culphert's orders.

I'll work harder, I thought as I walked away, yet I knew that I wouldn't. The best thing for me was to play music, to go to New York. When I was famous, then I could do whatever I wanted. Maybe in New York I would have a chance to be famous. I thought of my failed attempt to be a magician on the amateur talent show. In New York, whites weren't prejudiced against Negroes, were they? No! If I was a good musician, nobody would care that I was a Negro. No matter what Culphert would say about it, the main thing was that I should go to New York.

As the day approached, I told Dorothy that I was going to be working in the North and saving money for my school clothes, which would in turn save Culphert money.

I stayed out at Uncle Lofton's on the night that I was to leave for the North. The next morning I arose early and went out to the road and waited for Mr. Walker to pick me up. As I stood by the mailbox, I had the sudden fear that Culphert would come down the road and jump out of his truck and beat me. Then I saw a car coming down the road. It was so far off that I couldn't tell if it was Culphert's truck or Mr. Walker's Ford.

My heart beat with anticipation. Then, when it was close enough, I saw that it was Mr. Walker's Ford. Pulling up close to me, he smiled, and I ran over to the car and got in. In twenty minutes, we were out of Bolton and on our way north.

PART THREE

Make Voyages!

"Make Voyages, attempt them,
there is nothing else"
—TENNESSEE WILLIAMS in
Camino Real

Chapter 20

~~~~~~

My first view of New York was in the late afternoon. Twisting my neck, I leaned out the back car window and looked at the buildings. It was amazing. How tall they had made them. And what was it like to be in one of them?

On the way up, I asked Mr. Walker a thousand questions about New York, but all he would say was, "You'll see."

I couldn't stop looking at the people on the street. Some were white and some black. Nobody told the blacks they couldn't walk on the street. I saw a black man standing right next to a white woman who didn't seem to mind his presence.

As the car pulled away from a stoplight, I saw a black man with a red handkerchief around his sweating head pulling a cart down the street. He looked like somebody from our town. And that one, he looked like Geechie Collins. That one there, the white woman, why, that could have been Mrs. Harris!

We left Fifth Avenue and eventually passed through Harlem. People sat on the stoops and milled everywhere in the street. I would follow one interesting face only to lose it when another face, more interesting, seized my attention. I watched a woman walk past another woman, watched her behind and then watched another woman's behind, a car intervened, a child ran across the street, an impromptu dance broke out among a batch of kids, a snatch of music mingled with the heat and floated upward.

We drove from Harlem to the bridge and then to Long Island where it turned out Lee lived. The houses became sparser, more like a regular neighborhood, until we stopped in front of a two-story house.

I got out and Mr. Walker rang the doorbell. The door opened and a big woman with thin legs which seemed too thin to support her huge trunk, like a horse's body on donkey legs, came out and saw me and threw her arms open. "Morris! Come here, baby!" she cried out.

Feeling embarrassed, I spoke to her. She turned to Mr. Walker and said, "Thanks for bringing him," and took my suitcase and my horn and went back inside. I waved to Mr. Walker and followed her inside.

She made me supper and as she talked she explained to me that Uncle Isaiah and she were no longer together. He was living in Harlem somewhere, she said, with another woman. Of course, she said, I could go stay with him if I wanted to or I could stay with her.

I had no reason to want to see Uncle Isaiah, I said, not wanting to be more trouble. She showed me my room. I noticed that there was a backyard. There, I thought, I can practice my sax.

Later, at the dinner table, she took one look at my plate and asked me if I was finished.

"And what about that?" she asked, pointing to the pieces of bread I had left on the plate. "Honey, this is the North," she explained, picking up the bread. "You ain't living with Lofton and Amanda now. You can't just eat the white part of the bread. This is the North and if you gonna be living with me, you got to eat the crust of the bread too!" She was very serious. She was so stingy that she saved every bit of the crumbs and fed it to her little Chihuahua dog.

That Monday morning she took me to the factory where she worked. We went in to see the manager.

"Good morning, Lee-Ann," he said, as we came into his office. "Who is this?"

"That's my nephew I was tellin you about," she said. "He wants to work for the summer."

The white man got up and came around to look at me. He was a short, dark-complexioned man, and he chewed on a cigar stub.

"You ever worked in a factory before?" he asked me.

"No, suh—I mean, no sir!—I mean, no!" I stammered like my Uncle Sugarboy. I was suddenly aware that I had a southern drawl. Although Uncle Lofton had raised us never to say "yessir" and "no sir" to white people, I could not help myself from saying it to this little man, who for his part seemed astonished that I regarded him as a subject worthy of such respect.

"What are you? Some kind of plowboy?" the foreman laughed.

"No, sir!—I mean, no!"

"He's never been off the farm before," Lee said, sounding southern herself.

"Do you know how to do this kind of work?" he asked me.

"No, sir! I mean no!" I stammered again. And again, he laughed.

After a while, he winked at Lee and took the cigar out of his mouth.

"Okay, we gonna give you a try," he said, laughing. "But you better be a good worker. Come on, I'll show you what I want you to do."

He took me to the machines and showed me how to take the yarn from the storage warehouse and place it on the machines, according to size and color. As he took me to punch my card, he said to me, "This is your first time off the farm, eh?"

"Yes, suh—I mean, *yes!*" I said.

"Boy, you can't say 'yes,' without saying 'yes suh,' can you?" he said again. He seemed to have found my behavior strange, and this made me embarrassed. "Here," he said, sticking the card into the slot. "This is the time clock. This tells us how much you worked. Now, do that whenever you come in, and when you go out. Got that?"

"—Uh, yes!" I said.

"That's it, that's it!" he said, leading the way to the door. "Now, take the card and go to work."

I started to turn away, but he had forgotten to tell me how much I was earning.

"How much do I get?"

"Like everybody else who starts here," he said. "Two dollars and fifty cents an hour, and you work forty hours a week."

"Thank you," I said, and went to work. He was not as bad as I thought. He was like Elwood Martin, the other white man I knew well. I was proud of myself because I had managed to close the conversation with a simple "Thank you."

As I got the hang of the job, I felt awfully conceited. Man, I was really grown up. I was working in a real factory. I looked over the forty machines clacking and humming a whole new world that I felt I belonged to.

Lee came to watch me work and helped me when I put the blue bowls where only the yellow were supposed to be. "Don't ever do that," she said. "He gets mad about that." She sounded like Aunt Amanda when me and my brother worked at Smith's Anchorage Club. The black woman used her position to help the black men in the North as well as the South, I realized.

At lunchtime, I ate with a small group of men. I had never seen men like these. Some were Puerto Ricans, most were white, a few black. Some sat on boxes, while others shot craps in a circle in front of them.

"You just off the farm, huh?" one of the black boys asked me.

"Uh-huh!"

He laughed, but his laughter didn't embarrass me. I trusted it, because he reminded me of my uncles back home. He said his name was Peter, and he came from Georgia.

"Don't do that, man," he said, when he saw me paying attention to the crap game. "Don't *ever* play that. They will just take your money." Although he didn't know it, I had no interest in risking my money.

"Well, it was nice meeting you," I told him when I saw that it was time to get back to work.

"You'll be seeing me," he said, with a wry glance.

That evening as Lee and I drove home, she asked me if I liked the job.

"I like it," I told her.

"Well, when you get your paycheck, you got to pay me rent," she said.

I was surprised that she would want money from me, and I realized, suddenly, that people in the North were not like people back home, who would only ask a member of the family for money in order to survive.

"Okay," I agreed.

When we got home, I went to my room and unpacked my saxophone. I had played a few notes when the door opened.

"What the hell is that?" Lee asked.

"My saxophone."

"I can see that, Morris, but what you think you doing?"

"I was practicing."

"What about the neighbors? You think they deaf?"

I hadn't thought about that, since when I practiced at home, I practiced in the hay barn or out in the woods.

"Where can I practice?" I asked her.

"Practice? For what?"

I couldn't tell her that my secret ambition was to be a jazz musician. If I got a job playing jazz, I would never go back home. But I couldn't tell her that. Not now. "I mean, like, I have to practice . . ."

She looked at me, as if she was trying to make up her mind. "I don't want you disturbing these neighbors of mine," she said. "Don't play that thing in here."

"Yes, ma'am," I said and put it back in the case. I lay on the bed in the dark, miserable that I was not able to play yet feeling lucky to have a job. I would have to make enough money to find a place big enough so I could practice, I thought. An old abandoned warehouse would do the trick. I fell asleep dreaming about my future as a jazz musician.

I woke up when Lee called me to dinner. "If you want to play that thing," she said as we ate, "there is a room in the back. But don't blow that thing at night. If you want to blow it, do it in the afternoon."

"Okay," I said. She didn't know how happy she made me by saying that.

"And don't you want to visit Isaiah?" Isaiah lived in Harlem, and I had wanted to go to Harlem since I arrived but had no means to do it.

"Yeah," I said, "I would love to go visit him."

"Well, one of these weekends you should go over there and stay with him. I'll call him and see when he wants you to come."

"Thanks," I said, sliding from the table. I went straight to bed, excited to wake up the next morning to go to work.

The next day at lunch, I saw Peter again. "What you want to do up here?" he asked me as we ate our sandwiches together.

"I am a musician," I told him. "Not a plowboy."

He laughed. "Plowboy is a musician! What do you play?" I told him, and he laughed again.

"I am a musician too," he said. "I want to hear you play."

"Okay."

"You come by my house," he said, and told me how to get there.

The next evening, I found his house and rang the doorbell. "Come in, plowboy," he said. There were five other people gathered around a piano.

"Go ahead," one of the men called Lou said. "Play something."

I knew the solos from "There's a Thrill on the Hill," "Tequila," "Long Tall Sally," "You Better Shop Around," and other popular tunes I played with the Bebop Kings. I played the first solo and they listened quietly until I finished.

"Okay," Lou said. "He can play." Then the others started laying me compliments on my riffs.

Peter said, "Plowboy, we want you to come with us. We got a gig next week. But you have to practice with us first."

I was overjoyed when I left that day. I kept saying to myself, how lucky you are! You've been in the North only a week and you have a gig already!

The next morning, I got up early and wrote Uncle Lofton a letter. When Lee and I got our coffee and Danish, I bought a stamp and mailed the letter.

"Next week is your first paycheck," she reminded me. She complained about money all the time and made small notations about money she had spent on me, money I would have to pay her back as soon as I got paid.

That Monday, I went in with the line of people and picked up my check. It was for fifty-two dollars. I felt like I was rich. I gave Lee ten dollars "on the rent," as she described it, and the rest of it I put in a savings account, which she showed me how to do.

I took out enough for my food and some extra for when I went to visit Isaiah that weekend.

When Saturday arrived, Lee drove me to his place in Harlem. "Ike'll put you on the train Sunday night," she said to me as she drove off. Starting up the steps, I looked around at my surroundings. There was a gang of tattled black kids, my age, sitting on the stoop. They looked at me and I at them.

"Boy, where you from?"

"North Carolina," I said.

"Country nigger!" one of them shouted and they all laughed.

I ran on up to the apartment and rang the bell.

"That's the wrong bell, fool," another one said. "Ike live on the top floor!" I pushed the right button, wondering how they knew who I was visiting. How did they know that I was Ike's nephew, anyway? Was Ike's drawl so strong that they could identify us both by the country intonation?

"Hey, Morris!" somebody yelled, and I looked up to see Ike's big round face. "Come on in, boy!"

184

"How you doin," I asked him, stepping inside.

Uncle Ike grabbed me up in his arms in a bear hug. A pretty black woman stood next to him.

"Baby, this is that little nigger I been tellin you bout," he said, introducing us. "Hello," I said to Baby Doll.

Baby Doll was about three hundred pounds, with a sweet, child-like face.

"Hi, Morris," she said in a southern accent too. "I heard all bout you already, boy. Ike been tellin me all bout you and them magic tricks! Boy, you want a drink?"

"Go with Baby Doll," Ike said. "She gonna fix you up."

I followed Baby Doll to the kitchen where a pot of boiling chit-lins stunk up the place. A few people sitting at a table greeted me as we passed. She poured me some corn liquor from a mason jar and shoved it to me.

When the chitlins were ready, we sat down to eat, and the door opened and a couple of women, loudly dressed in bright red and green, rushed in talking a mile a minute about what had just happened to them on the street.

When they finished their tales of escape from the police, the danger resolved into loud laughter and long swigs of liquor in celebration of their survival. I gathered that they were prostitutes and found them interesting.

Soon the apartment was filled with men in wide-brimmed sum-mer hats with bright headbands. They sat around the big table playing cards all night while the women kept coming and going.

Uncle Ike was a gangster, I could tell, from the way he kept all these beautiful women around him. He would dart in and out of the apartment, and his girlfriend, Baby Doll, big and fat, would waltz in on a serene cloud of marijuana.

Eventually, I started going to Uncle Ike's every weekend. Dur-ing the week, I would work and practice with Peter and his friends. The gig we were practicing for was still a week away. I realized that playing with these guys wouldn't lead me to the big league, but I was willing to play with anybody until somebody introduced me to something better.

Chapter 21

~~~~~~

At one of Uncle Ike's parties, I saw a couple of white guys. I started talking to one of them whose name was Barney.

Although he didn't seem much older than me, Barney had graduated from college. He told me later that he and his buddy bought some "weed" from Uncle Ike. It made sense to me, since Uncle Ike seemed to be doing something illegal.

I followed Barney around for a while on the weekends and soon learned to puff on a stick of marijuana with him. He took me to his parents' house in New Jersey where he pointed to the wall on which his Columbia College diploma hung.

"I can't read it," I said, looking at the strange writing on it.

"It's Latin," he said, laughing. "I don't know why, but it's written in Latin. It doesn't mean anything, but I got it."

Besides being the first white person I knew who had a college degree, he was further distinguished by being the first white artist I ever knew, or certainly one of the first people I'd ever known who went around telling people he was an artist.

"What are you going to do?" I asked him, while we were in his room.

"I want to sculpt," he said. He showed me large pieces of rock that he had been chiseling on.

"They pay you a lot of money to do it?"

"No," he said. "I don't care about the money, I just want to be an artist."

This inspired me, because I wanted to be an artist too.

A big, buxom woman came into the room with a tray of sandwiches. "Are you from Columbia, too?" Barney's mother asked.

"No-ma'am—I mean, yes!"

His mother glanced at Barney quickly and then glanced back at me. "You ain't from Columbia?" She seemed surprised, as if all the boys her son could conceivably associate with must come from Columbia.

"He's from the South," Barney said, pulling his hands through his beard.

His mother gave me another look. "Oh," she said, and left the room abruptly.

She didn't come out until we were about to leave. Barney had rented a car and told his mother he was going to drive up north to a college to visit a girl. She asked me if I was going to drive the car too.

"I don't know," I said. I didn't even know that I was going.

"Do you have a license?"

"Yes!"

She made me take it out and show it to her; but when we were going out the door, she seemed as uncertain as before.

"Be careful, Barney," she said. "And if he drives, tell him to be real careful." She was, to my surprise, talking about me right in front of me, as if I could only be communicated with through her son.

When we were driving down the road, Barney laughed. "That's a Jewish mother for you!"

I laughed. It was the first time I had ever heard of a "Jewish mother." Somehow, I liked her, though. I was fascinated by the way she never listened to anybody but kept repeating the same thing over and over again, no matter what the response was.

Instead of driving to the country as he had led his mother to believe, Barney drove down to Greenwich Village. I admired the way he had lied to his mother. It was so natural.

We sat in a cafe which was full of beatniks. At a coffee table, I sat in astonishment and watched a beatnik reading poetry. He was black and wore a black beret. When he finished reading his poetry, which was about how much he hated his father, the audience applauded and he went back to sit at a table with a white woman.

As I got to know the Village better, I discovered black men who were painters and saw other blacks who sang and played jazz. I felt a deep emptiness every time I saw a black man with a bebop cap on his head and a saxophone mouthpiece between his lips, because that was what I wanted to be.

I thought I had met such a person when I met Rufus, an old man who played saxophone too. I met him through Peter. Peter told me to meet him under the El on 125th Street in a bar there. I waited there with my horn. While I was waiting this old man came up to me and asked me if I had a sax in the bag. When I told him I did, he asked me if I was pretty good. I said, "I can play it a little bit." I always said it like that because you never know how good the guy who asks you is. If you make him think you are not so good, then he will be in for a surprise when he hears you.

So it got around to me asking him, and he said the same thing. "I play a little bit," he said.

Suddenly while we were standing at the bar, I got the weird notion that this old man could really play. Maybe he was a genius like Coleman Hawkins. So I said, "I'll play something and you play something!" Being slick. Bringing him out.

So I took my horn out, put the mouthpiece on, and blew a riff.

He said, "That's good!" So then I passed the horn to him. He placed the mouthpiece in his cracked lips and blew a riff that was so beautiful that I almost flipped. He played something else that took my breath way. Who was he? Was he a famous musician? I wondered.

"Oh, that sho is pretty, Rufus," the woman working the bar said.

Rufus looked at me. "Where you from?"

"North Carolina. Bolton."

His eyes widened.

"I'm from North Carolina, too."

"Yeah?"

"Ever heard of High Point?"

Reverend Harvey Bourne's people were from High Point.

"Yeah!" It was unbelievable to meet a black man from someplace I knew who could blow a horn like that.

"That's where I'm from, yessir, many years ago, though," he said, thoughtfully. I looked at his raggedy clothes. Certainly a famous musician down on his luck. But why? I wanted to be a musician, but I didn't want to look the way he did.

"Did you ever meet Coleman Hawkins?" I asked him.

"Yeah," he said as if he didn't want to discuss it further. "I played with him."

My eyes must have gotten pretty big, because he shook his head and said, "Look, Youngblood, you like to play, good? Don't ever think of making a livin out of this. It will only break your heart!"

What he was trying to say to me was that I'd end up like him.

"Are you gonna play soon?" I said.

"No, I'm too rusty," he said.

"Why don't you practice a little?"

He laughed. "They took my horn." He was too broke to own a horn.

"If you teach me to play like you, you can use my horn."

"Well," he said, disguising his modesty, "I don't know that much to teach, but I'll teach you what I know."

I left my horn with him, with the promise that we would meet the next day and he would show me a few things.

The next day I went to the bar and waited for him.

"Have you seen Rufus?" I asked the woman working behind the bar.

"Rufus?" she asked. "What you want to see him about?"

"My saxophone," I said. "I lent it to him."

She leaned over the bar and stared down at me. "You what?" she demanded seriously.

"I lent him my horn," I repeated.

She shook her head and turned to a man at the bar. "This poor chile lent his horn to Rufus," she said sadly. The man looked at me.

"Man, you'll never see that horn again!"

Suddenly I felt funny. I didn't know why, but suddenly I had a feeling I never had before. Even when Culphert beat me, I didn't feel this way. I felt something was missing inside, a feeling that wouldn't go away. Even before the woman began to explain, I knew what she was going to say.

"Honey," she said, taking me to the end of the bar. "Rufus is a junkie. You ain't never gonna see your saxophone again. He done pawn it to get him some dope! Now, you just done go and trust no junkie . . . see, he plays good, but he is a dope fiend . . . and you a *country* boy . . ."

"It's a damn shame," the man sitting at the bar commented again, glancing pityingly at me. I made it outside somehow and

walked down Eighth Avenue. It was the first time I had been so
open to a stranger, and I had been shot down. A black man had
done this to me. Why had a black man done this to me? My
saxophone was a symbol of my effort to escape the oppression of
my father. Why had I trusted him in the first place? In a blunder,
I let an old black man rip my magic shield from me.

I walked and studied that sea of black and brown faces—faces
that floated by in waves of humid hot air. The dull, lost hope in
their eyes depressed me. My suffering made their suffering real.
I realized that these people were as much victims of the white
man as we were in the South. Why had Rufus taken my horn?
Because he needed heroin. Why did he need it? Because he
couldn't get a job. Why couldn't he get a job? Because the white
man in the North was no different from the white man in the
South.

All the qualities I admired in Rufus—his reticent glib jive talk,
his phrasing on the sax, his way of being—I now rejected. I floated
with the flow of the black crowd, letting them pull me along. Now
I saw the meaning behind Rufus's words to me, "Don't ever try to
make a living out of it. It'll break your heart."

He was trying to warn me against people like *himself*! I had
been too young to hear what he was saying. Now I paid the price
for my innocence.

I began to think about my situation as belonging to the situation of all black people, North and South. I hated Rufus as I hated
my father, and the faces of the people around me became one with
these two faces. The frustration in the faces of the black men who
passed me now was the same frustration I had seen in my father's
face. I began, suddenly, to understand my father's face, and I
began to see and to understand why he had been so mean and
brutal to me. Perhaps he had not been brutal enough.

He was only treating me like Rufus was treating me. My father,
however, bought me a horn, but Rufus stole it. I hated the black
people in the North for disappointing me. My father had suffered,
but compared to the northern blacks, he had been one of the lucky
ones. I had thought I was mistreated in the South, but now as I
looked up at the blacks hanging from the fire escapes in the siz-
zling hot summer sun, at these walking zombies, I realized that
I was one of the lucky ones, too.

From this time, I hung out in the Village, and I started imagin-
ing myself not as a black musician any longer, but as a poet. I

liked the image of the black hipsters reading their works. And their themes, "Fuck the society," "Fuck the Father," appealed to me.

One night, Barney invited me to a party not in the Village, where we usually went, but up near Columbia, on the West Side. The poets and writers and beatniks I had seen in the Village were there too, but there were also other types which I had not seen before.

I met a young white girl who stood all evening surrounded by tall, white-complexioned young men wearing glasses. They were discussing Pound, Eliot, and other poets I had never heard of. "What do you do?" I asked her.

"I am a translator," she said with a French accent. "What about you?"

"I am a writer," I said, surprising myself. (I couldn't say I was a musician; the pain of that memory was too much.) I had been drinking and said the first thing that came to my head.

"What did you say?" She leaned closer to me, and I wanted to reach out and touch her. But I realized then why she was leaning toward me. Having had a few drinks, my speech had reverted back to the despised southern dialect. I was sounding just like a country nigger.

"I want to be a writer," I said, embarrassed that she would not believe that I could be a writer from the way I sounded.

"Oh, that's wonderful," she exclaimed, and instead of seeing through my ignorance, she began to talk about some famous writer who was her favorite.

Barney slipped up beside me and said, "Get her telephone number." Why? I wondered. Did he want to call her? She was beautiful and white, so I didn't think I could call her up. Where would I take her? What would we talk about?

But when I went for a drink, Barney came up to me again.

"She's beautiful, get her number."

"Why?"

"Call her up!"

"But I live with my aunt on Long Island."

"You can take her to my place."

I went back to her.

"Could you give me your telephone number?" I stumbled out shyly. "I could call you."

"Oh, sure," she said. I was so astonished. My face was hot and

191

I felt nervous as I reached out to take it. She smiled and said, "Call me."

"Did you get it?" Barney asked, and when I said yes, he beamed with pride and slapped me on the shoulder.

"You never slept with a white woman, huh?" He laughed, seeing how it made me so upset. I was ashamed that I was nearly a virgin.

"Come on, let's go! These people," he said, as we walked past another white girl surrounded by white men, "they don't like Negroes here."

Northerners *had* to like Negroes, I thought, watching them angrily. How could they dare not like us when the southerners were hating us. So this is what they had been talking about all evening! I looked at the girl and now I understood—I thought— why the men were standing around her. She didn't like me and she was talking to them about me.

Forgetting my embarrassment about being a southerner, I walked up to her. "Why don't you like Negroes?" I asked her to the corner of her face. I saw her face turning, saw her look of surprise, but I didn't care. I was angry.

"Why do you ask me that?" she asked, startled. I hated the way she and her friends appeared to me: intelligent, snooty, hip. I started telling her about how white people should leave the black people alone.

"What do you think about the bus boycott in Mississippi?" she asked me. She knew all about the sit-ins and boycotts all over the South and in some northern cities. I didn't know all what she knew but I was the very thing she had been reading about in the papers. I was the sharecropper's son.

"Come with me, I want to get another drink. We can talk."

She got a drink and we talked and drank and smoked cigarettes. She was the first person who seemed really interested in the details of my life without making me feel ashamed of myself.

She told me her name was Sophie and that she had two desires—one was to be an actress and the other was to be a civil rights worker in the South.

"Let's go outside and get some air," she suggested, and as we left the party, I could feel the stares of the white boys she had been talking with.

When we were outside she hailed a taxi, and we went to her

apartment. This was the first time I had even been alone with a white girl, except with Jill, when she watched me feed the pigs. But that was so long ago and we were so little that it didn't mean anything.

It was easy to be with Sophie. I talked and talked, and she poured drinks and lit cigarettes and listened. She had books all over the apartment, with plants, just like a grown-up person, although she was not yet twenty-one. She was older than me, but it didn't matter. Nothing mattered but sleeping with her.

Her father was a liberal, she said, and the only black people she knew were the two who worked for her father in the house. She asked me about my life and I told her.

Sometimes she would interrupt me and ask me if I'd read a certain book. "Do you know James Baldwin's book?"

"No," I said.

"You should read it," she said, handing me the book from her shelf. "It's just about what you were saying."

I took the book. "Thanks," I said. I had the feeling she knew more about me than I knew about myself. I felt ashamed and insecure.

"My high school is not so good," I said.

She touched my arm. "That's alright," she said. "What's important is that you can change it."

She was so encouraging that I kept wondering why Barney told me she hated Negroes. She told me about herself. She went to college, a girls' college, and her father was a writer for a newspaper in Newport. She majored in English. When she went to get some ice, I saw that she had the same book that Barney had been carrying around, *Journey to the End of the Night*, on her shelf.

After I had another drink, she asked me what I wanted to be.

"I want to be a writer," I said, remembering that it had gotten a big reaction out of the other white woman.

"That's what I thought," she said, so naturally.

"Why?" I asked, but she responded only with laughter.

"When you write a book will you put me in it?" she asked. It was such a funny question that I didn't know what to say to her. Maybe this experience would turn out like the one with Rufus, where he tried to warn me against him, while at the same time trying to con me.

"Sure, why not?" I said, draining my glass. It was late, and I had not thought about Barney, nor had I thought about how I was going to get home.

"I'm hot," she said.

I had heard the expression and definitely knew what it meant, but I sat there just looking at her, not being able to believe that she was saying it to me. We looked at each other and I knew that it was going to happen. She was so open to me that I felt like a bird let out of his cage. My fantasy was to be with a white woman alone, and to be freed from my own sexual desire.

I leaned down and kissed her. I thought that she was letting me do it. It did not occur to me that she was realizing one of her fantasies of sleeping with a southern Negro.

We didn't laugh or smile, but clung to each other with kisses and touches. When I reached down to touch my cock, I felt the sticky juices where I had already ejaculated. My uncles told me that before making love, you should masturbate so that the juices would not make the penis go soft. Without the juices, the penis could be like wood a long time.

The excitement gave me a long hard-on, with no ejaculation juice left. When we made love, I felt the rhythm of making love to her and became in touch with the mystical feeling I had when I worked in the field, casting all of my earthly feelings aside.

We slept late that Sunday morning. Then, when we got up, she made coffee, and we sat at the table, glancing through the *New York Times*. I felt so grown-up, like a man, a real man. Sleeping with a white woman made me feel I had reached manhood.

"If you write the way you make love," Sophie said to me, teasingly, laughing, with a piece of toast in her mouth, "you will be a great writer."

We made love again before I left, and when I came out of the apartment and walked down the street, I felt like a man. Sophie! She was the most important person in my life.

When I got home, Lee looked at me. "Where you been all weekend?"

"I was at my best friend Barney's."

"What you doing with him?"

"He's just a good guy. He's okay."

"You better think about who you are running around with in New York."

I went and threw myself across the bed and opened the book Sophie had given me to read. I was still looking through it when the phone rang in the next room. Lee's footsteps approached the door, which she pushed open.

"Somebody wants to talk to you!" Talk to me? I couldn't imagine who it could be.

"Happy birthday, Morris!" It was my mother.

I was shocked and delighted, shocked to realize that I was so far away from home, the distance being confirmed by my mother's din of a voice and the sad tone in it, and delighted that they had remembered my birthday.

"Dorothy, hello," I said.

"Everybody misses you down here. They all wants to know if you getting rich."

"Hey, how is everybody?"

"They is fine. Are you minding Lee-Ann?"

"Yes, I'm minding her."

"Do you like it up there?"

"Oh, yeah."

"Now remember you be back here for school."

I told her that I was saving my money and that I would certainly remember to come back. I asked about Uncle Lofton. She said he was fine and asked if I wanted to speak with him. Uncle Lofton came to the phone. I was ecstatic. His voice was so distant and yet so near. He asked me how I was doing. I told him how much I liked it up here. That was good, he said, but I should come back and finish school.

"How's Aunt Amanda?"

"She's right here, trying to break the phone out of my hand."

Aunt Amanda came on the line and told me about some pies she baked, reminding me of the good cooking that awaited me when I returned home. After I had talked to her for a while, she gave the phone to somebody else. The familiar sound of the voice sent a pain through my stomach.

"Hey, boy, how you?"

"I'm okay."

"You doin alright?"

"Yes sir."

It was Culphert. He said I was still under his "jurisdiction" until I was eighteen. He asked me if I knew that he had the legal right to have a truant officer pick me up and bring me back to Bolton. Did I realize that?

"Yes, sir, I do."

Did I think that I could walk over him? No, I didn't. Why hadn't I asked him for permission to go to New York—why hadn't I acted like a son who respected his father? I tried to remind him that I *had* asked him, but he shouted me down with another question: did I believe that I could get away with my total disregard for his authority, just because my mother, my uncle, and aunt had all conspired together to aid me in stepping over him? No, I told him, I didn't believe I could get away with it.

"You damn right, you won't," he said. "I want you back in Bolton at my house on the first day of September. Do you understand that?"

"Yes, sir."

He gave the phone to my mother, who said I shouldn't pay anything he said any attention. "He gets that way sometime, like you know he do," she said, but long after he had hung up the phone, I couldn't get the hostile ringing of his voice out of my head.

Chapter 22

The Greyhound bus was full of black people on their way home to the South at the end of the summer. A few white passengers rode up at the front of the bus. It was a few days before the first of September, and I was headed home.

A black elderly woman sat next to me with big, bulging packages for her grandchildren. She had lived in Harlem for a few years working as a domestic. Now she was returning to the South.

When the bus pulled onto the New Jersey Turnpike, I opened Sophie's present, the last thing which would remind me of her. It was a book called *The Young Writer*, by Jesse Rader.

I looked out the window and thought of my summer, of those weekends I went to see Sophie. When I was visiting one weekend, she asked me if I liked Chinese food. When I told her I had never eaten Chinese food, she leaped up in bed.

"You've never eaten Chinese food?" she asked, as if it was a big deal. I told her I had never eaten Chinese food, and I didn't see the reason for her astonishment. In fact, what I didn't tell her was that I had never heard of it.

"I can't believe that," she said, shaking her head with laughter. "He's never had Chinese food." And then she looked at me. "Get dressed. We gonna get some Chinese food."

We went to the Village, which wasn't far, since she lived on Eighth Street, and walked into a Chinese restaurant.

When the waiter brought us the meal she ordered, I couldn't believe the color and smells. Sophie watched me every time I tasted something new, and when I showed excitement and surprise, she would laugh out loud. She had a great time just watching me eat.

The next weekend, she turned to me after we made love and asked, "Museums? Ever been to a museum?" Would I like to go to the Metropolitan Museum?

Then one weekend, it turned out very badly. I knew something was wrong when I saw, as I came up the stairs to her apartment, one of those tall, eyeglassed white boys who had been standing around her at the party coming down the stairs. I started to speak but he rushed by me like I was a plague. I went on upstairs and rang at her door.

When she opened the door she looked depressed. "What's wrong?" I asked her when I got inside. She stood before me and dropped her head.

"Nothing," she said. I put my arms around her, smelling her wonderful scents. She let me kiss her and I pulled her down on the bed. She let me rub her thighs like she always did, but I could tell something was wrong.

"Say, was that one of your friends from the party going down the stairs?"

"Yes," she said. "He's mad with me."

"About what?"

"About you," she said sadly.

"About me?" I was astonished that I had caused a problem between them. "Is he mad with me?"

"No, he's mad with me," she said, and kissed me again.

"Why?" I didn't understand why he should be angry with her and not with me. That my having sex with her was a problem to a white man didn't bother me. But what irritated me was her boyfriend's strange way of reacting to my sleeping with her. Why didn't he come right out and call me a nigger and try to beat me up, if not kill me? But his sulking away without confronting me bothered me.

"For this," she said, pulling me back on the bed.

"Does he love you?" I asked.

"Yes," she said. "He said forever."

"Do you love him?"

"I don't know," she said. Then she looked at me from the side of her face. "Do you love me?"

I was embarrassed because I thought Sophie regarded me as

198

the sexual experience I had regarded her. I was a bit surprised that she took her emotional feelings for me so seriously.

"Yes," I said, not believing it, but saying it because I was put on the spot. But did I love her? What I felt for her was more than love, certainly more than I could say. What could I tell her? She had given me the first feeling I had of being a man with a woman. I was grateful to her for that, but what could I tell her? I had ejaculated with women before, but this was the first time I felt a woman wanted to make love with me in a full-size bed.

I looked over her apartment, at her books, her plants, at her long blond hair. No, it was something more than love. It was admiration, amazement, an incredible experience that would take me a long time to unravel.

"Yes, I love you," I said again.

"I love you, too," she said. "And I don't care about Jeff anymore." I pulled her close to me and we made love right there on her bed.

I touched the book as if I were touching her. Outside the window the city was slipping away from my view, faster and faster. Would this feeling I had about Sophie pass, too? Was it possible to love a white person?

The bus arrived that afternoon in Wilmington. I got off and waited for my mother to pick me up. I waited for her about an hour before I realized that she had been standing in the next room waiting for me. I saw her through a window in the partition that separated the blacks from the whites. She was standing about five feet away.

"Dorothy!"

She turned and saw me.

"What the hell you doing waiting over there!" she said, and pointed to a sign.

I looked at the sign and saw that it read WHITE ONLY.

"I didn't see the sign," I said, as we walked to the car.

"You didn't see the sign?" she asked. "But you saw the white people, didn't you?"

"What white people?"

"All them white people there!" She pointed to the other side of the room. Yes, she was right. There were white people on one side of the building and on the other side of the wall were the black people.

Segregation was a fact of life in North Carolina in 1960, but I had never really noticed it before. Now I gazed at the black people, dark and sullen, huddled together in the shabby-looking room on one side of the station and the whites, coolly omniscient of their power over us, spread out comfortably in the green chairs.

Had I gone to the WHITE ONLY side unconsciously? Perhaps? Had I unconsciously used it as a signal to my mother that I had changed? By allowing her to find me in a sea of white faces, wasn't I telling her that my worldview had changed?

I did not want to insult my mother, yet it seemed inevitable. She believed that whites had a benevolent side to them, but this, as far as I could see, was an illusion which Negroes had to cling to, because, like all illusions, it justified their unwillingness to change their situation.

Yet I realized that my indifference to the Jim Crow rule was a wedge that I could drive between me and my parents.

Dorothy was seeing something in me she had never seen before, and perhaps it frightened her. I remembered thinking of the time she had slapped me for kissing Jill's hand, I remembered her way of teaching me to never be attracted to white women.

"What you want to be with the white people for?" she would ask, as if I had turned into some kind of monster.

"Dorothy, what difference does it make?"

"It makes a lot of difference! You better not let Culphert see you do nothing like that."

"Like what? Who the hell is he?"

"Hell! You cussing me now, boy!"

"No, Dorothy, I'm not cussing you."

She didn't even ask me anything about my trip. She and I began to fight for the first time in my life.

"You can't be yourself no mo," she said, as we drove across the Wilmington bridge to the flatland which passed through three townships—Leland, Armour, and Acme—before it came to our own Bolton.

The drawbridge, which had seemed so large before I left, seemed so small to me now. I looked down at the water—damn, it was only a few feet up, big enough to let a little tugboat pass under it.

It was a clue to what was coming. The town, as Dorothy drove into it, depressed me with its smallness. Dorothy would say later, "Nothing pleased him. He was dissatisfied with everything!"

I looked at A. J. Harris's store and it looked just like the one in Money, Mississippi, where Emmett Till had said "Bye! Baby" to that white woman who (from the pictures Sophie and I found in a book) looked just like Mrs. Harris.

I now felt guilty about sleeping with Sophie. What would happen to me if some white man down here found out about it? What could stop them from doing to me what they did to Emmett Till who, like me, had come down to the South from the North? And Emmett Till had an excuse that I didn't have: he didn't know the ways of the white people, he was not from around here as I was.

We passed through Bolton, past Bertha Long's place, the white woman we sharecropped for, past the white Davis place, and past the Lomax place; it was like being lowered slowly into hell. I felt depressed, humiliated, and afraid.

As the car turned into the gate, I saw Elaine, Brenda, Cornelius, Donald, Fred, and the Baby Vivian all rushing to the porch.

They jumped on me, pulling me and shouting as soon as I got out of the car. I was happy to see them. Fred was about five years old. He kept pulling my arm and saying he had seen me in the sky.

"Where?"

"Up in the sky," he said, pointing to the sky. "Dorothy, didn't I see Morris?"

Dorothy laughed and explained, "He thought that when you went up north, you went in an airplane. He came running in the house, saying, 'Dorothy, I think I saw Morris.' I said, 'Where, Fred?' He said, 'Up in a airplane.' I said, 'Did you really, Fred?' He said, 'I believe so.'"

Elaine, about twelve, grabbed my bag to carry it into the house and had to fight Donald and Brenda for possession of it. Because I had been up to New York, I was a celebrity.

"Where's your saxophone?" Knee asked me loud enough for Dorothy to hear. I pretended not to hear him, but he repeated until I told him I left it in New York. "You'd better not tell him that," Dorothy said. "He gone fly off the handle if he hears that."

"I don't care what he fly off of," I shouted back at her.

"Now lissen to him," Dorothy said. "Just as mannish as he can be. What you smellin youself now? Wait till that man gets home."

I went to my room and unpacked my bags, surrounded by my

brothers and sisters, all of whom were clamoring for stories about New York.

It was still in the afternoon. I went with my brother to the barn so we could talk.

"I got something for you," I told him.

He had been watching the bebop straw cap I was wearing. I had two of them, and I gave one to him. He was delighted with the hat, and this pleased me. I was happy to see him again and was eager to rekindle our old childhood friendship immediately.

After a while, I heard Culphert's truck driving up. I braced myself as I heard him take his place at the dinner table. Then my mother called me to eat.

Chapter 23

I came into the room. Nobody spoke to me as I took a seat at the table. Culphert sat across from me, sipping coffee from the blue jay china saucer, blowing on the hot coffee, cooling it.

"Next week we oughta start disking those corn stalks down in the swamp."

"Yah," I said, too depressed to fight back.

That was the end of the conversation. He didn't say a thing about my trip. It was as though I had never been away. I left the table as soon as I could.

In my room I sat on the bed, stunned. How could I get away? Get away forever! What I hated was that he still treated me like I was a country plowboy who had never left the farm, and who had never been to New York. I had been in the North, which was more than you could say for him! Stupid, ignorant convict!

The next morning, I got in the truck and drove down to the farm.

Pulling the truck up to Big Bertha's yard next to her old Ford, I cut off the engine, opened the door, and slid from the seat. I could see the unplowed fields that Knee and I worked from sunup to sundown for four years.

As I came to the screened porch, I saw the porcelain statue of a grinning Negro servant that I hated so much. With its grotesque grinning face, its lips curled up in a perfect servile, bootlicking gesture, the fawning emblem demanded my attention.

It seemed to me that the inanimate object was alive. Out of those contorted black lips came the words, "Hey, hey, boy, you can go to New York, but you still come back to me! You and me will always be together! Boy, we tighter than fish pussy, and that's waterproof!" Oh, how I would like to smash it in a thousand pieces!

Stepping up to the door, I rang the bell.

"Yais, cain I help you?"

I turned and looked into Big Bertha's face. Her face, wrinkled like an orange left too long in the sun, hung cautiously between the opening in the screen door. She was older, even though it had only been a few months ago that I had worked for her. Was it that my perception had changed, and now I was seeing her for what she really was? She used to be strong, but now she was like a cripple.

"Culphert wants to see if I could borrow your disk."

She looked me up and down slowly, not as if she didn't believe me, but as if she had not heard what I said.

"Oh, you're Cuffy's boy," she said, as if her senses were coming back to her.

"Cuffy's boy," I said. I hated her so much at that moment, I could have reached over and killed her without the slightest remorse. Why was it that, in this goddamned town, no matter how old you became, white people still identified you as your father's child? Wasn't it because of slavery, where the slave was always the property of the slave master? And here she was saying I was the property of Culphert?

"Yeah," I said, my voice brimming with contempt, "Cuffy's boy!"

"Yais," she said, pretending that she didn't notice my hate. "How's yo daddy? I guess he sent yo over to borrow that two-blade disk, I reckon."

"That's right," I said, knowing that she expected a "yes, ma'am."

She cracked the screen door wider, looked at me, and then pulled the door close.

"Yeah, Cuffy's boy!" I thought, glaring over at that grotesque Negro, who was still glaring at me, as if he were now saying to me, "See, nigger, ain't nothing changed! She still doesn't see what she has done to you! You still my little nigger if you don't get no bigger!"

Suddenly I had an idea. Nobody would see me if I gave that ugly grinning nigger a push. I leaned over to see if she was watching me through the screen door.

I shoved my hand into his fat, ugly nose, and the statue tumbled backward speechless as the famed tar baby and, hitting the hard cement walkway, shattered into a million pieces.

Old Bertha wasted no time getting there.

"That was really an accident," I said, disguising my laughter behind my hand.

"Lord, you done damaged a precious antique!" she squawked.

She stood looking down at the scattered pieces, and she started crying.

"That was an antique. An antique, priceless antique!" She slammed the door, and I went off to the shed to get the disk.

When I got home, Culphert was waiting for me, furious.

"What can I trust you to do, Morris?" Naturally, she had phoned him. "You went an destroyed that white woman's precious antique."

"It wasn't an antique and it wasn't precious. It was an Uncle Tom statue."

"Hell, I know that, but you should be more careful. You know who these white people are."

I thought he would be even angrier.

"Come on," he said. "Let's go."

"Where?"

"We got to go buy her another one."

"What? You kiddin?"

"Get in the truck, boy."

We drove all the way to Whiteville to a yard with a sign over it, STATUES MADE HERE. How was it possible that my own father, who could kick my ass for the slightest thing, was such an Uncle Tom to this racist bitch? How? He would actually go to all this trouble to replace her racist statue!

I watched him and a white man pick out another one of those ugly things. I stood there, surrounded by ugly servile Negroes!

"Boy, come here!"

I went over.

"Ain't that the one?"

On the way back, he said to me, "If she had called the law on you, she would be within her rights. You can't destroy people's property!"

"Her property? But what about my own rights?"

"Your rights?"

"She is calling me an inferior person by just having that statue in her yard."

"Well, I guess you think cause you went up to New Yawk, you can just walk over people!"

I could sense the violence in his voice, but I was determined not to let him hit me again. If he hits me, I told myself, we are going to tumble.

I was silent, but this didn't satisfy him. He changed his tone of voice.

"I'm proud of you, Morris," he went on, driving back to deliver this piece of shit. "I am proud of what you have achieved. I never went to New York, never had the chance. But I don't want to say that I was not smart enough, I think I was. And you are smart enough. I just didn't have the opportunity. You know about the trouble I was in. Now I know you didn't intend to destroy that woman's property, but you *did*. That's a fact! Right or wrong, you got to see when you do something wrong to other people. Now put yourself in her shoes. Regardless of how racist she is, and I'm not saying she ain't, how would you feel if she had knocked your statue over?"

"In the first place, I wouldn't have something that stupid in my yard."

"Irregardless of that!"

"But I did."

"What?"

"I did destroy her property. I was *trying* to destroy it. I did it on purpose."

"Is that what you learned in New Yawk, son? To hate?"

"White people hate us," I said. "They hate us!"

"Don't nobody hate nobody," he said.

How I despised him! He had become the person the whites said the black man was. He was afraid of this old broken-down white woman, and I hated him for it.

When we got back to Big Bertha's, she and Culphert stood with the statue between them and reestablished their former relationship. They talked about me like I wasn't leaning there on the truck.

"That was an antique," she growled.

"This one is an antique, too," he said, carrying it over to where she was standing. "Is this where it was?"

"Leave it there, Cuffy."

"This boy of mine apologizes for that accident." Culphert was grinning better than the statue. Why didn't Big Bertha just keep him?

"That ain't the one," she said, looking at it.

"Not the one?"

"The other one had a red jacket on. He was a little old jockey. But this one is holding a bridle. The other one was not holding a bridle."

"I thought that boy told me this was the one."

I was laughing, because I had deliberately told him wrong.

"No." She was shaking her head. "This is not the one."

Culphert said, "I'm going back to Whiteville tomorrow, and I'll take it back and get the right one."

"Leave it. I don't want to put you to no more trouble. I know how these young people are. When you want to do something, you might as well do it yourself."

This meant that Culphert had been restored to his former position of a good nigger in her eyes.

"Well, you know he's been to the North," he said, meaning that I could be excused for being an outsider. "And he never was cut out for this kind of work. Farm work."

Oh, I was glad to hear that!

"I can change that antique and get the other one," Culphert offered again.

"Don't worry about it," she said, and she looked down at the statue. "I'm getting to like it already." She smiled at Culphert, and said, "Get that disk anytime you want to, Cuffy. Just bring it back when you finished."

She hobbled on back into her house.

Just as we pulled through the gate into the swamp, I saw a group of white men standing around a truck. As we got closer, I saw their expensive hunting clothes and the dogs and their rifles with telescopes on them. A truck with specially built doghouses stood on one side of the road. This was a hunting party that Culphert allowed to hunt on our land because it was so fertile and full of deer. But if this had been Elwood Martin's land and we wanted to hunt on it, Elwood Martin would have charged us a lot of money to do so. Why didn't Culphert charge these white men money for hunting on our land? Hadn't my Grand Papa Cecil worked hard to get it? Why had Culphert been so subservient to the whites?

As we drove closer to the hunters, Culphert slowed down the truck and Elwood Martin, dressed in bright red hunter's gear, came over to him.

"Cuffy," he grinned, as Culphert slid out of the truck, "you just missed a big buck!"

"Did you get him?"

"Missed him," one of the other hunters said. The other hunters came up to meet Culphert and they all laughed together just like they were friends. I stood there hating them all, because I had hunted with Lindsey who didn't need any fancy outfits or telescopes to kill a deer, and now that Lindsey was dead, and killed by a white boy, it made me angry to see Culphert even talk with them, to say nothing of letting them hunt on our land!

As we drove on to the farmhouse Culphert slowed the truck down. "I want to talk to you about your future, Morris," he said, pointing out the window suddenly. "See that field over there," he said. "I've decided that I want you to have that when you graduate from high school."

I could tell from the tone of his voice that he wanted me to be thanking him, but I held back.

"I know you think I've been mean and hard on you and your brother, but that's because you don't understand the situation as I do. Now you got to realize that life is hard on you because you are a black and I want to give you this land so that you can at least have a place to build you a house. When you got a house, nobody can tell you to move and if you're going to have a family that's the most important thing."

I didn't say anything. He stopped the truck and we got out and he started walking across the field to the empty house and I followed him.

"Do you understand what I'm talking about?" he asked me.

"What I don't understand is why you let Elwood Martin hunt on our land and not charge him?" I asked him, afraid that he would hit me or slap me for being so bold. But I figured that if he was going to talk seriously to me about my future and about my grandfather's land, then it was alright to tell him what was on my mind.

I was surprised that he didn't hit me but took my question seriously as if I was a man like him.

"Yeah, that's right," he said. "I should charge them."

"They would charge us," I said, eager to express my disapproval of how he treated white people with respect when he knew they never treated us with respect.

"If Elwood had the swampland where all the deer are, and if

we had that flatland that he has, he would make us pay a lot of money to hunt his deer. But we got it, so we should make them pay!"

"That's the way you think now because you went up north," he said. "But that ain't the way you suppose to be with people. I am a Christian and I want Elwood to see that I don't have to charge him. I want him to see how I can give to him without begrudging him!"

"But he don't think that. He just think that he's taking advantage of us!"

"Well, if he got that kind of heart, that ain't my business. My duty is to be respectful to him! If he don't know how to return the favor that ain't my business!"

I was furious with him for this point of view, but I didn't say anything. We walked on further until he stopped. "This land here I am going to give to Knee for his house."

"But why do you want us to live down here?" I asked him.

"You don't have to take the land, if you don't want it," he said. "I'm giving you the choice. If you want to farm with me, then you can have this land. I'm going to do by you the way Cecil did by me. He bought this land so that we wouldn't have to be under the white man, and I'm giving you boys your inheritance the same way that my daddy gave me."

"But I don't want to live down here in the swamp," I said.

He turned to me. "When I was your age, I hated the farm, too. I married your mother and went to the North, hoping I would never have to be a farmer. But it didn't work out that way. After I got in trouble and was in prison, I had to come back to the land. But thank God, I had this land to come back to. If I hadn't had this land, I would have to be living up north somewhere. And who knows what I would have done then? Who knows how I would have been able to take care of you and your brother?"

And beat us? How had that helped, I thought but was too afraid to say it to him. Was that necessary? To beat us and make us work so hard?

We had come to a clearing. Culphert stopped and pointed to the pine trees ahead of us.

"All these woods are going to be cut," he said. "That's why I brought you here to show you what I've done. Do you know what I've done?"

I didn't know what he was talking about.

"I've made the decision to lease this land, about three hundred acres of land, to the Riegal Paper company," he said, "for ninety-nine years. We will all be dead when it comes back into the Brown family." He turned to me again.

"This land will belong to your grandchildren, a long time after we are dead. That's why it's important that you have children, because this is your grandfather's land."

"How much money are you going to get?" I asked him.

"More money that I thought I'd ever get," he said.

"What do you want me to do?" I asked him.

"I want you to work with me," he said. "And you won't have to worry about money for the rest of your life."

"But I want to go to college," I said.

"If you stay with me," he said, "I'll guarantee you that you will be able to go to college. I'll give you the money to pay for it."

After our walk we drove back home. I went straight to Uncle Lofton and talked it out with him. I asked him why Culphert still wanted to keep me on the farm. "Why doesn't he just let me go!"

"See now," Uncle Lofton said. "Culphert's a little jealous of you."

"Jealous of me?"

"Fact is, he is a lot jealous of you."

"How? How could he be jealous of me?"

"See now, he was the one who wanted to be smart. Now he went up there with Dorothy and tried to make it and didn't. But you might make it, you have a chance to do it."

Could it possibly be true? Was there something that I had that Culphert envied in me? When he had taken a trip up north, he had ended up in prison. Had I succeeded where he had *failed*?

"Daddy, I don't want the land," I said. "And I don't want the money that he will give me to send me to college."

"I know you don't," Uncle Lofton said.

"Daddy, I'm still afraid of him," I told him. "I don't want to be around him."

"I know that, but he is your father," Uncle Lofton said. "But now that he's going to get that money, maybe he will change."

I remembered the violence and the beatings and I knew I wouldn't feel I had fulfilled my life if I stayed in Bolton with Culphert, even if he was going to be rich. I knew that if I left to go north everybody would think that I was throwing away my future. I didn't know what to do.

That night I lay in bed thinking about my life—about Sophie, New York, the sax, and my ambition to be somebody. School would start in a week. I wanted to do well this year, this year of my last chance. I wanted to do well, because my father could not help me. I could see plainly now how bitter he had become. I couldn't go back to the North, not after what had happened to me with Rufus. There were too many Rufuses waiting for me there.

Chapter 24

〜〜〜〜〜〜〜〜〜〜〜〜〜〜〜〜

I called Randell on the phone to get the lesson assignments for school so that I would not be so far behind. I had missed class for a few weeks because I had been working with Culphert, helping to haul tobacco to the market and plowing up the tobacco stalks.

"We gonna have the scholarship examinations tomorrow," he told me.

"What exams?"

"The scholarship examinations," he said.

"To go to college?"

"Yes."

"How did you know?"

"Mr. Corbett passed a list with everybody's name on it who will take it."

"My name wasn't on it?"

"No!"

"Mr. Corbett didn't put my name on it?"

"No."

I was angry. This was one of my chances to get out of this hell! The examination for a scholarship? It seemed so unbelievable that fate had so arranged my life that I would miss the scholarship examination. How could I be so unlucky. I hung up the phone, not knowing what to do.

The next morning, I had to plow the field until eleven o'clock, but I couldn't take it any longer. I tied the mule to the tree and gave him some hay and hitchhiked to Armour to see Mr. McNeil.

When he saw me crying he knew that he had to do something. "Why didn't he put my name on it?" I cried.

"He doesn't think you are college material," McNeil said. "He has other students in mind that he thinks should go to college."

That hurt me even more than the fact that he hadn't put my name on the list. Although it might have been because I couldn't come to school all the time, I read many more books than most of the other students. "But why doesn't he think I'm college material?"

"I believe in you," Mr. McNeil said. "I believe you can do it. I'm going to talk to Corbett for you."

So he went to see the principal.

"What can I do?" Mr. Corbett said. "The boy is not college material."

"But I think Brown has the ability to pass high on the examination," Mr. McNeil told him.

"How can he take the examination now?" Mr. Corbett said. "The school bus that takes them to Wilmington left this morning."

Mr. McNeil shook his head. "That doesn't matter," he said. "I can drive him up there."

"You can drive him up there?" the principal asked, leaning across his desk in disbelief. "What about teaching your classes?"

"I can get somebody to teach them."

"Okay, if you feel that strong about it," Mr. Corbett said finally, "go ahead."

Mr. McNeil came back and told me what had been decided; I was delighted. Mr. McNeil decided to lend me his car to drive there. Leon Lloyd went with me. As we drove up to Wilmington, I was afraid that I would disappoint Mr. McNeil, but at least I would have a chance to take the examination.

We arrived at the examination room just in time for me to take a number. I stood looking over the large classroom at the rows of students before I took my place. I thought about Uncle Lofton and Mr. McNeil and Mr. Adams and Miss Laws, my English teacher, before sitting down at the desk. I hoped I wouldn't disappoint them.

As I walked away from the exam, I was plagued with doubt. But at least I had taken it. I had not been defeated by my father this time. I had taken it, in spite of him.

The next day I was back in the field plowing Big Red and the exam faded from my mind. When I came back from the field, my mother was talking about Billy Pyatt being sentenced to ten years in prison for raping Helen Lomax.

"That's what that crazy nigger deserve," she complained from the stove. "Jumping on that woman like that!"

"But Dorothy, how do you know he did it?" I asked her. I knew, also, that there was gossip that Billy Pyatt had not raped her, that she and Billy Pyatt had been "going together," as the people described it, for a long time and that she and Billy Pyatt had been caught by Helen Lomax's daughter Jill.

"What you mean? You know he did it! These niggers round here is crazy bout white womens!"

I couldn't tell her that I had slept with a white girl in the North. She would not even be able to understand how I could have loved Sophie.

"Don't you go telling lies like that on Helen Lomax," she said. "I know these trifling niggers round Bolton. I know they just want to believe that Helen would do a thing like that. I don't believe it!"

"But Dorothy, you don't know what she was doing all the time," I protested. "How do you know that she wasn't going with Pyatt?"

"I don't know, but I also know how low these niggers is in this devil's hole, too!"

"Why do you think Billy Pyatt would jump on her," I said. "Maybe she jumped on *him*!"

Dorothy turned on me with a look in her eye which was meant to chasten my imprudence. "And what do you mean by that?"

I dropped my stance and turned to the door. "Nothing," I said, and went to my room.

The next day at school, Mr. Adams, my agricultural teacher, told me to stay after school.

"Brown, we need to think about what you want to do after high school," he said. "There is two new factories being built. Do you think you'd like to talk with somebody from there? They are going to be hiring young men like you."

Mr. Adams was right. Riegal and Dupont representatives had begun to contact teachers at our school. For many black students this was the highest job they would ever dream of having.

"I'll think about it," I told him.

I kept thinking about it all the way home. I took the school bus home and got off and walked up to the Hill Farm. I realized that the only way out of my situation was to go to college, but if I couldn't do that, I had three options. First, I could work in the Riegal plant or the Dupont plant. Both of them were chemical plants that took the trees which covered our county and chewed them up into fabric which made paper. Leon and Booty and Kenneth Melvin and most of my friends were going to work in one of these two factories. They would marry their girlfriends and have children and nothing would change for them that would be different from what had happened to their parents.

Second, I could go up north and take my chances in getting a job. But I had already been up north, and I kept the picture of Uncle Ike in my mind. That would be disastrous for me. I would end up in jail. I would be on the street like all those other blacks I saw in Harlem. I dreaded to be like so many of these blacks who had no self-respect, no dignity, no money. The idea of living in the squalid conditions of the northern Negroes depressed me even more than the idea of working in the factories.

Third, I could stay on the farm with Culphert and work with him. He would give me a piece of land and I would find a girl to marry and I would live in a new house which I would build and have children as he had done. This would mean that all my efforts to escape since I was a small child would have been in vain. Whatever it was that oppressed me about my father would now take its full toll on me.

I still hoped that I would get a scholarship. I believed that I had done well on the test, but I wasn't sure at all.

One afternoon when I came in from school Dorothy told me that "something from some college" had come for me. "A letter, Dorothy?" I asked her.

"I don't know," she said. "You have to go out to Lofton's and see."

I jumped on my bicycle and rode to Uncle Lofton's. The letter was on the table. I opened it. It was from the Agricultural and Technical College in Greensboro, North Carolina, and I had been awarded a scholarship to attend college because my test scores had been so high.

I sat there and read that letter over and over again before I told anybody about it. The letter stated that I would be awarded a scholarship for the academic year of 1961–62.

When Uncle Lofton came home, I showed him the letter and told him what it meant.

"Daddy," I said, "I can go to college now!" I grabbed him and hugged him and Uncle Lofton was so happy that he started crying. When Aunt Amanda came home from the Smith's Anchorage, she cried, too. She got on the phone and called her brother, Culphert, and told him that I had a scholarship to college. I didn't even talk to him after that, because he knew that I would not work for him any longer, even if he was the richest man in the world.

I went up to the Hill Farm; Dorothy was happy when she saw me. She wanted to know when I was leaving. I told her the date on the letter was September; she and Aunt Amanda started packing my bags in June.

There was an article in the school paper about my winning the scholarship. Of all the students who had taken the examination, only James Randell, my best buddy, and Thomas Jacobson and I won a scholarship. Even though it was in the papers, Aunt Amanda told the good news everywhere she went.

Aunt Amanda bragged to Mrs. Harris about me. Then she told me, "That boy of hers didn't get in a college. He's going to jine the army."

We all knew that for a white boy to join the army and me to be going off to college was a major victory.

Our school graduation was a modest ceremony. It was held on Sunday, May 21, 1961, in the school gymnasium. Aunt Amanda sat on one side of me and Dorothy sat on the other side. Behind us Uncle Lofton waited. He rarely went to anything, but he said he wanted to come to this because I had gotten a scholarship.

We all had to stand and sing the hymn "Come, Thou Almighty King." Rev. J. W. Wilson gave the invocation, and then the Glee Club sang "My Desert Flower."

When our principal introduced the guest speaker, I became aware that the speaker was the dean of A & T College, the college which I was to attend. At the end of his speech, he said, "Three scholarships have been awarded to Thomas Jacob, James Randell, and Morris Brown."

When my name was called, I turned to look at Aunt Amanda, and tears were rolling down her cheeks.

Dr. Robinson's commencement speech was full of good advice, hope and promise for the future. I listened to it all, and believed it all. Yes, I would succeed, I told myself, and silently I repeated to myself my resolve to be a writer.

After Dr. Robinson had taken his seat, Mrs. Corbett, the principal's wife, presented us with our diplomas. We had to stand in a line behind the stage. As I stood waiting for my turn, I watched Randell as he reached for his diploma with the right hand and shook Mrs. Corbett's hand with the left. I will do what Randell did, I thought; he was always right.

I went up and got my diploma from Mrs. Corbett. When I came down on the other side of the stage, all the parents were there. My mother was standing there smiling at me as I came down. I came up to her and gave her a hug, and she kissed me on the cheek.

"I'm so happy for you," she said. "At least you got through high school!"

"Dorothy, you'll see," I promised her. "I'm going to get through college, too."

Daddy was standing there. "Well, Morris," he said, "I'm glad you got more education than I ever got. I hope you use your education so that you won't have to work as hard for your living as I did. That's all I want for you!"

Mr. Corbett came down the stairs after the ceremony. I went over to him. Mr. McNeil looked at me and smiled. "Mr. Corbett," I said to him loud enough so that Mr. McNeil could hear me too, "I did get a scholarship after all!"

"Yes, Brown," he said, his teeth clenching the cigarette holder. "I knew that you could do it!"

Mr. McNeil winked at me and shook his head. Dr. Robinson, Mr. Adams, and Miss Laws all looked over at me proudly. The Glee Club was singing the triumphal march from "Aida," and I was very happy.

I spent the summer working in the field, plowing Big Red, but I did it with pleasure for I knew that it would be the last time I would plow a mule.

When the time came for me to leave home, Aunt Amanda and Uncle Lofton drove me all the way to Greensboro in their new car.

217

My mother had my bags packed with a chicken dinner to eat when I was alone up there in the dormitory.

Just as we came out of the road, I saw Culphert's truck coming up the road. We had to stop the car.

"Go say good-bye to your daddy," Aunt Amanda said. I had to get out of the car and go over to his truck.

"I'm proud of you," Culphert said, getting out of the truck.

I didn't know what to say. He had a package in his hand which he handed to me. It was so heavy that I asked him what was in it.

"I bought that for you," he said. I opened it to see a typewriter. "If you're going to be a writer," he said, "you got to have something to write on, don't you."

I heard my Aunt Amanda say behind me, "Now, ain't that just what he needed!" She loved her brother and it was just perfect for her that he had given me a present and wished me luck.

"Thank you," I said.

"I don't know nothin else, son," he said. He had given me my first musical instrument, and now he was giving me a typewriter.

"But that's alright," I said, just wanting to get away. His display of emotions embarrassed me.

"Good-bye, Morris. I did the best I could."

"Good-bye," I said, and turned to the car.

As the car drove away and they disappeared from my sight, I thought of my father's nightmare which was his life. I thought of that morning when he woke up and discovered he had killed a man.

I turned my head back from the town and set my eyes on the road up ahead.

Coda

~~~~~~

There is Doulichion and Same, wooded Zakynthos,
but my island lies low and away, last of all on the water
toward the dark, with the rest below facing east and sunshine,
a rugged place, but a good nurse of men; for my part
I cannot think of any place sweeter on earth to look at.

—Odyssey, IX 24–29

It was pitch-black when I arrived in Bolton, the night before
Christmas of 1990, but by the headlights I could still pick out all
the important markers from my childhood days. My plane from
San Francisco landed in Charlotte and from there I took a rented
car. An hour and a half later, I was in Bolton—population 563. I
was on the road to Outback to Uncle Lofton and Aunt Amanda's
place.

There was my Grandfather Cecil's house, remodeled as a split-
level brick, now occupied by my Uncle Elmo, and there on the
right was our first grammar school, and a mile further, on the
right, Lee's Chapter Baptist Church, where I first remember hearing about Jesus walking on the water.

Across from the church, there on the right, was Reverend
Bowen's house. It was here in this house that he and Mrs. Betty
had raised his eleven children. I slowed down so I could see the
house clearly. Recently, Bolton was on prime time news, the first
time in its history. Bolton's first black mayor, Sidney Bowen, had
been shot down in his yard by a state trooper for allegedly drinking
a beer. State Highway Patrol Trooper Alfred E. Morris stopped
Mr. Bowen in his front yard, chased him around his house,
brought him back to the front yard, handcuffed him, beat him

with his flashlight, and when Mr. Bowen tried to defend himself, the trooper pulled his .9mm and shot him five times in front of his wife and daughter.

Sidney was the boy who told me Aunt Amanda had got him a job. Sidney my childhood friend. As I stood, I reflected on the fact that thirty-one years ago I left this town to go to college. Had I stayed, there was the possibility, too, that I could have ended up like Sidney Bowen. The truck which Sidney was driving was still parked in the driveway. In the glare of the headlights I saw an old tree behind the house. It was in this tree, forty years ago, that Sidney and his brothers Felton and Otis and my brother raided a blue jay's nest for the eggs on a Sunday when we should have been in Sunday school.

I drove two hundred feet more and came to my road. As I drove down the poor unpaved road to my father's house, on my left side was Reverend Bowen's tobacco field where Felton had now built a large brick home. In a few seconds, I was pulling up in the yard.

Uncle Lofton and Aunt Amanda, now in their seventies, were still the same. Daddy and I embraced. Aunt Amanda insisted on my sleeping in my old room, and when I went to my room, I discovered that much of it was the same. Even though several nephews had occupied my room over the years, the bureau was still filled with my old school materials, my magic books, and secret devices for vanishing silks and cigarettes.

At breakfast, Daddy and I talked about the past, enjoying all the old stories. When I asked about Smilin' Henry and Carl Mack, he said, "They jes drifted off . . ." Elder Townsend? Had he just drifted off too? "Drifted off where? Naw suh! Elder Townsend ain't gon nowhere!" Uncle Lofton told me. "You know he must be a good preacher if these people ain't run him off after forty years!"

The first impression I had of the town was completely different from what I remembered. As I looked for the green trees that I remembered, what I saw was a brown, treeless, uninteresting little town. There were no more farms. Middle-class brick houses with neat lawns were springing up everywhere. When I was growing up here, those houses were fields of green corn, waving in the breeze with tall pine-leaf trees standing in the background.

I was happy to see my real mother. Culphert and Dorothy live in a comfortable brick house built shortly after I left home. Culphert placed a trailer next door to the house, where he lives most of the time.

I went over to see him in his trailer. I told him how his beating me had affected my life, that I still have fear of him, and as I reached out to hug him, he pulled back a bit. But then realizing that he shouldn't fear me, he allowed me to give him a hug. I couldn't talk to him about my pain without crying. I had left my father's nightmare very far behind. I did not believe, as he had believed, what whites said about me, that I was inferior simply because I was black. I told him how much his life had hurt me. I told him I wanted to get rid of the demon that his life had caused me. I asked him to tell me what had happened that Saturday night.

During the war, he said, the shipyard at Wilmington closed down and they got word from somebody that they were hiring in Portsmouth, Virginia. He moved with my mother and me, where we lived in the Carver Homes, a cheap housing complex for war-time shipyard workers.

Like most blacks who had recently migrated from the tobacco fields and turpentine swamps of the Carolinas, my father and his friends worked all week and gambled and drank on the weekends. There were many fights, but the next day, Sunday, when they had slept off their drunk and were sober, they were friends again. This was survival for underclass blacks during wartime.

In a card game, he got into an argument with Robert, one of my mother's first cousins. The rest of the men joined in against him. He remembered how he ran home through a bean field to get his gun. When he got home, my mother and Sylvia, who sometimes cared for me and my nine-month-old brother, tried to stop him. In any case, he couldn't find his pistol. But on his way out the door, he grabbed the ice pick from the ice block.

As he started back across the field, he encountered some of the men. Another fight ensued. Robert wasn't with them, but his brother George, who had tried to stop the fight, was. When George fell, the others jumped on my father. One of them drew a pistol into his face and was about to pull the trigger when Tootsie, my mother's brother, begged him not to kill him.

The last thing he remembered was that somebody hit him with a two-by-four, and Tootsie carried him home, where he had fallen into a drunken daze.

That Sunday morning, as he was waking up and about to get out of bed, he heard my mother and her cousin Sylvia sobbing. There was a knock at the door. It was the police with handcuffs.

George was dead. Culphert had killed him, my mother's favorite cousin. His own drinking buddy and friend. He had killed George.

When he finished I sat there wondering why he couldn't have told me this earlier in my life. But this inability to communicate with his children was part of his crime. I told him how relieved I felt to have him tell me in his words what had happened to him. He said he understood and he was sorry that it caused me so much pain.

That night I went to meet a few of my high school friends, Leon Lloyd, Willie Lloyd, Sam White, all who were in the band Bebop Kings. We met in Bubba Bland's place, a garage he has turned into a place where he sells liquor by the paper cup, and the only form of formal entertainment is a portable radio.

The noise level was loud, and in the excuse of Christmas spirits and my homecoming the liquor went down quick.

They told me that Billy Pyatt worked as an orderly in a resting home. Henry Lomax divorced Helen. Junior Pyatt stayed in jail for several years, still not saying a word about what happened. Henry got cancer, and went down to the jail and begged the judge to let Billy Pyatt out of jail, which they did. But Henry died anyway. Right now the daughter Jill is married with three children and is living in the old Hill Farm where we used to live.

My last visit was with Mr. Roy. He now lives in a trailer in Bolton. Mrs. Suzanne sat at a table and was being fed by one of her daughters. In the next room, Mr. Roy Melvin sat on a bed surrounded by young teenagers and a few older black men, most of whom were in my grade level at school.

I got Mr. Roy Melvin to play the "Fox Chase" on his harp. "Go, boys, go," he'd always say, and I imagined myself, among the other children, dancing as fast as I could.